ENDOMETRIOSIS COOKBOOK

MEGA BUNDLE – 5 Manuscripts in 1 – 200+ Recipes designed for Endometriosis diet

TABLE OF CONTENTS

BREAKFAST 12
PINEAPPLE PANCAKES 12
ALMOND PANCAKES 13
APPLE PANCAKES 14
STRAWBERRY PANCAKES 15
PEAR PANCAKES 16
LETTUCE OMELETTE 17
ZUCCHINI OMELETTE 18
JICAMA OMELETTE 19
MUSHROOM OMELETTE 20
BASIL OMELETTE 21
MUSHROOM OMELETTE 22
BREAKFAST MIX 23
SAUSAGE BREAKFAST SANDWICH 24
BREAKFAST GRANOLA 25
PANCAKES 26
BANANA PANCAKES 26
PINEAPPLE PANCAKES 27
ALMOND PANCAKES 28
APPLE PANCAKES 29
STRAWBERRY PANCAKES 30
PEAR PANCAKES 31
COOKIES 32
BREAKFAST COOKIES 32
SMOOOTHIES 33

FIG SMOOTHIE 33

POMEGRANATE SMOOTHIE 34

GINGER-KALE SMOOTHIE 35

BERRY YOGHURT SMOOTHIE 36

COCONUT SMOOTHIE 37

RASPBERRY-VANILLA SMOOTHIE 38

CHERRY SMOOTHIE 39

CHOCOLATE SMOOTHIE 40

TOFU SMOOTHIE 41

ORANGE SMOOTHIE 42

RAISIN DATE SMOOTHIE 43

MUFFINS 44

SIMPLE MUFFINS 44

GINGERBREAD MUFFINS 46

CHERRIES MUFFINS 48

BLUEBERRY MUFFINS 49

BERRIES MUFFINS 50

CHOCOLATE MUFFINS 51

RASPBERRIES MUFFINS 52

SECOND COOKBOOK 53

BREAKFAST RECIPES 54

PANCAKES 54

BLUEBERRY PANCAKES 55

ALMOND PANCAKES 56

BANANA PANCAKES 57

STRAWBERRY PANCAKES 58

SIMPLE PANCAKES 59

GINGERBREAD MUFFINS 60

BANANA MUFFINS 62

BLUEBERRY MUFFINS 63

STRAWBERRY MUFFINS 64

CHOCOLATE MUFFINS 65

SIMPLE MUFFINS 66

BERRY FRENCH TOAST 67

POHA WAFFLES 68

BREAKFAST BISCUITS 70

INDIAN PANCAKES 71

COOKED MILLET 72

MUFFIN MIX 73

BANANA BREAD 74

FRITTER 76

HOT CHOCOLATE MIX 78

PANCAKE SYRUP 79

PINEAPPLE BREAKFAST CAKE 80

SCRAMBLED EGGS WITH RICE 81

TART RECIPES 82

APPLE TART 82

CHOCHOLATE TART 84

PIE RECIPES 85

PEACH PECAN PIE 85

BLUEBERRY PIE 86

PUMPKIN PIE 87

SMOOTHIE RECIPES 88

GREEN SMOOTHIE 88

WAKE UP SMOOTHIE 89

RASPBERRY SMOOTHIE 90

CHOCOLATE SMOOTHIE 91

PROTEIN SMOOTHIE 92

SUNSHINE SMOOTHIE 93

MANGO SMOOTHIE 94

PEACH SMOOTHIE 95

PUMPKIN SMOOTHIE 96

ICE-CREAM RECIPES 97

COFFE ICE-CREAM 97

STRAWBERRY ICE-CREAM 98

THIRD COOKBOOK 99

SIDE DISHES 100

FRIED VEGETABLES 100

ONION SAUCE 102

FISH "CAKE" 103

SUSHI HANDROLLS 104

STEAMED VEGETABLES 105

GUACAMOLE 106

CHICKEN NACHOS 107

SCRAMBLED EGGS WITH SALMON 108

CHICKEN WITH RICE 109

ROASTED VEGETABLES 110

SAUSAGE PIZZA 111

HEALTY PIZZA 112

SLAW 113

EDAMAME FRITATTA 114

ONION FRITATTA 115

LEAF FRITATTA 116

KALE FRITATTA 117

JICAMA FRITATTA 118
BROCCOLI FRITATTA 119
CAULIFLOWER SANDWICH 120
AVOCADO BOATS 121
MEXICAN CORN DIP 122
LEEK QUICHE 123
ROASTED SQUASH 124
BRUSSELS SPROUT CHIPS 125
CUCUMBER CHIPS 126
SQUASH CHIPS 127
PASTA 128
SIMPLE SPAGHETTI 128
SHRIMP PASTA 130
PASTA WITH OLIVES AND TOMATOES 131
SALAD 132
MORNING SALAD 132
TOMATO SOUP 133
CRAB SALAD 134
ASIAN SALAD 135
CHICKEN SALAD 136
CUCUMBER SALAD 137
GRAPEFRUIT SALAD 138
APPLE SALAD 139
COLESLAW 140
LOBSTER SALAD 141
RADISH SALAD 142
SPINACH SALAD 143
FOURTH COOKBOOK 144

SOUP RECIPES 145
   CAULIFLOWER SOUP 145
   MUSHROOM SOUP 146
   ZUCCHINI SOUP 147
   CELERY SOUP 148
   CARROT SOUP 149
   CUCUMBER SOUP 150

SIDE DISHES 151
   GOAT'S CHEESE RAREBIT 151
   SMOKED MACKEREL PATE 153
   PESTO CREAM VEGGIE DIP 154
   CAULIFLOWER CHEESE 155
   PUMPKIN RISOTTO 156
   GREEN PESTO PASTA 157
   MINCE WITH BASIL 158
   PORK CHOPS 159
   BEEF BURGERS 160
   BAKED FISH 161
   MINT COUSCOUS 162
   FRESH PORK PATTIES 163
   POTATO SALAD 164
   LEBANESE BEAN SALAD 165
   KALE & FENNEL SALAD 166
   TOMATO & SPINACH SALAD 167
   WILD RICE SALAD 168
   KALE SALAD 169
   THAI MANGO SALAD 170
   HERBED SALAD 171

BEET SALAD 172
PEPITAS AND CRANBERRIES SALAD 173
FIESTA SHRIMP 174
CAULIFLOWER FRITTERS 175
FRENCH TOAST SANDWICHES 177
GREEK MIXED VEGETABLES 178
GRILLED SALMON STEAKS 180
ORIENTAL GREENS 181
BROCCOLI CASSEROLE 182
BEAN FRITATTA 183
ROASTED SQUASH 184
POTATO CHIPS 185
PIZZA 186
ZUCCHINI PIZZA 186
TUSCAN PIZZA 187
MARGHERITA PIZZA 188
SHAKSHUKA PIZZA 189
FIFTH COOKBOOK 190
ROAST RECIPES 191
ROASTED SQUASH 191
ROASTED CARROT 192
SOUP RECIPES 193
ZUCCHINI SOUP 193
SIDE DISHES 194
CHICKEN NUGGETS 194
BEEF FAJITAS 195
SUMMER SALMON 196
GRILLED SALMON 197

MONKFISH MUSSEL KEBABS	199
POTATO TORTILLA	201
ASIAN STIR-FRY	202
APRICOT CHICKEN PATTIES	203
GREEN PESTO PASTA	204
SALMON WITH ROSEMAY	205
MUSHROOM BURGERS	206
BLACK BEANS BURGERS	208
CABBAGE FRITATTA	210
BRUSSEL SPROUTS FRITATTA	211
CELERY FRITATTA	212
PROSCIUTTO FRITATTA	213
OREGANO FRITATTA	214
HUMMUS WRAP	215
POTATO WEDGES	216
KALE CHIPS	217
EGG ROLL BOWL	218
GREEK BOWL	219
CRANBERRY SALAD	220
GAZPACHO SALAD	221
RADISH & PARSLEY SALAD	222
ZUCCHINI & BELL PEPPER SALAD	223
QUINOA & AVOCADO SALAD	224
TOFU SALAD	225
PAD THAI SALAD	226
AVOCADO SALAD	227
MUSHROOM SALAD	228
MIXED GREENS SALAD	229

QUINOA SALAD	230
STEW RECIPES	**231**
FISH STEW	231
BUTTERNUT SQUASH STEW	233
CASSEROLE RECIPES	**235**
BACON CASSEROLE	235
ENCHILADA CASSEROLE	237
PIZZA RECIPES	**239**
CASSEROLE PIZZA	239

Copyright 2020 by Noah Jerris - All rights reserved.

This document is geared towards providing exact and reliable information in regards to the topic and issue covered. The publication is sold with the idea that the publisher is not required to render accounting, officially permitted, or otherwise, qualified services. If advice is necessary, legal or professional, a practiced individual in the profession should be ordered.

- From a Declaration of Principles which was accepted and approved equally by a Committee of the American Bar Association and a Committee of Publishers and Associations.

In no way is it legal to reproduce, duplicate, or transmit any part of this document in either electronic means or in printed format. Recording of this publication is strictly prohibited and any storage of this document is not allowed unless with written permission from the publisher. All rights reserved.

The information provided herein is stated to be truthful and consistent, in that any liability, in terms of inattention or otherwise, by any usage or abuse of any policies, processes, or directions contained within is the solitary and utter responsibility of the recipient reader. Under no circumstances will any legal responsibility or blame be held against the publisher for any reparation, damages, or monetary loss due to the information herein, either directly or indirectly.

Respective authors own all copyrights not held by the publisher.

The information herein is offered for informational purposes solely, and is universal as so. The presentation of the information is without contract or any type of guarantee assurance.

The trademarks that are used are without any consent, and the publication of the trademark is without permission or backing by the trademark owner. All trademarks and brands within this book are for clarifying purposes only and are the owned by the owners themselves, not affiliated with this document.

Introduction

Endometriosis recipes for personal enjoyment but also for family enjoyment. You will love them for sure for how easy it is to prepare them.

BREAKFAST

PINEAPPLE PANCAKES

Serves: **4**

Prep Time: **10** Minutes

Cook Time: **20** Minutes

Total Time: **30** Minutes

INGREDIENTS

- 1 cup whole wheat flour
- ¼ tsp baking soda
- ¼ tsp baking powder
- 1 cup pineapple
- 2 eggs
- 1 cup milk

DIRECTIONS

1. In a bowl combine all ingredients together and mix well
2. In a skillet heat olive oil
3. Pour ¼ of the batter and cook each pancake for 1-2 minutes per side
4. When ready remove from heat and serve

ALMOND PANCAKES

Serves: **4**

Prep Time: **10** Minutes

Cook Time: **30** Minutes

Total Time: **40** Minutes

INGREDIENTS

- 1 cup whole wheat flour
- ¼ tsp baking soda
- ¼ tsp baking powder
- 1 cup almonds
- 2 eggs
- 1 cup milk

DIRECTIONS

1. In a bowl combine all ingredients together and mix well
2. In a skillet heat olive oil
3. Pour ¼ of the batter and cook each pancake for 1-2 minutes per side
4. When ready remove from heat and serve

APPLE PANCAKES

Serves: **4**

Prep Time: **10** Minutes

Cook Time: **20** Minutes

Total Time: **30** Minutes

INGREDIENTS

- 1 cup whole wheat flour
- ¼ tsp baking soda
- ¼ tsp baking powder
- 1 cup mashed apple
- 2 eggs
- 1 cup milk

DIRECTIONS

1. In a bowl combine all ingredients together and mix well
2. In a skillet heat olive oil
3. Pour ¼ of the batter and cook each pancake for 1-2 minutes per side
4. When ready remove from heat and serve

STRAWBERRY PANCAKES

Serves: **4**

Prep Time: **10** Minutes

Cook Time: **20** Minutes

Total Time: **30** Minutes

INGREDIENTS

- 1 cup whole wheat flour
- ¼ tsp baking soda
- ¼ tsp baking powder
- 1 cup strawberries
- 2 eggs
- 1 cup milk

DIRECTIONS

1. In a bowl combine all ingredients together and mix well
2. In a skillet heat olive oil
3. Pour ¼ of the batter and cook each pancake for 1-2 minutes per side
4. When ready remove from heat and serve

PEAR PANCAKES

Serves: **4**

Prep Time: **10** Minutes

Cook Time: **30** Minutes

Total Time: **40** Minutes

INGREDIENTS

- 1 cup whole wheat flour
- ¼ tsp baking soda
- ¼ tsp baking powder
- 2 eggs
- 1 cup milk
- 1 cup mashed pear

DIRECTIONS

1. In a bowl combine all ingredients together and mix well
2. In a skillet heat olive oil
3. Pour ¼ of the batter and cook each pancake for 1-2 minutes per side
4. When ready remove from heat and serve

LETTUCE OMELETTE

Serves: **1**

Prep Time: **5** Minutes

Cook Time: **10** Minutes

Total Time: **15** Minutes

INGREDIENTS

- 2 eggs
- ¼ tsp salt
- ¼ tsp black pepper
- 1 tablespoon olive oil
- ¼ cup cheese
- ¼ tsp basil
- 1 bunch lettuce

DIRECTIONS

1. In a bowl combine all ingredients together and mix well
2. In a skillet heat olive oil and pour the egg mixture
3. Cook for 1-2 minutes per side
4. When ready remove omelette from the skillet and serve

ZUCCHINI OMELETTE

Serves: 1
Prep Time: 5 Minutes
Cook Time: 10 Minutes
Total Time: 15 Minutes

INGREDIENTS

- 2 eggs
- ¼ tsp salt
- ¼ tsp black pepper
- 1 tablespoon olive oil
- ¼ cup cheese
- ¼ tsp basil
- 1 cup zucchini

DIRECTIONS

1. In a bowl combine all ingredients together and mix well
2. In a skillet heat olive oil and pour the egg mixture
3. Cook for 1-2 minutes per side
4. When ready remove omelette from the skillet and serve

JICAMA OMELETTE

Serves: **1**
Prep Time: **5** Minutes
Cook Time: **10** Minutes
Total Time: **15** Minutes

INGREDIENTS

- 2 eggs
- ¼ tsp salt
- ¼ tsp black pepper
- 1 tablespoon olive oil
- ¼ cup cheese
- ¼ tsp basil
- ½ cup jicama
- 1 cup red onion

DIRECTIONS

1. In a bowl combine all ingredients together and mix well
2. In a skillet heat olive oil and pour the egg mixture
3. Cook for 1-2 minutes per side
4. When ready remove omelette from the skillet and serve

MUSHROOM OMELETTE

Serves: 1
Prep Time: 5 Minutes
Cook Time: 10 Minutes
Total Time: 15 Minutes

INGREDIENTS

- 2 eggs
- ¼ tsp salt
- ¼ tsp black pepper
- 1 tablespoon olive oil
- ¼ cup cheese
- ¼ tsp basil
- 1 cup mushrooms

DIRECTIONS

1. In a bowl combine all ingredients together and mix well
2. In a skillet heat olive oil and pour the egg mixture
3. Cook for 1-2 minutes per side
4. When ready remove omelette from the skillet and serve

BASIL OMELETTE

Serves: **1**

Prep Time: **5** Minutes

Cook Time: **10** Minutes

Total Time: **15** Minutes

INGREDIENTS

- 2 eggs
- ¼ tsp salt
- ¼ tsp black pepper
- 1 tablespoon olive oil
- ¼ cup cheese
- ¼ tsp basil
- 1 cup tomatoes

DIRECTIONS

1. In a bowl combine all ingredients together and mix well
2. In a skillet heat olive oil and pour the egg mixture
3. Cook for 1-2 minutes per side
4. When ready remove omelette from the skillet and serve

MUSHROOM OMELETTE

Serves: **1**

Prep Time: **5** Minutes

Cook Time: **10** Minutes

Total Time: **15** Minutes

INGREDIENTS

- 2 eggs
- ¼ tsp salt
- ¼ tsp black pepper
- 1 tablespoon olive oil
- ¼ cup cheese
- ¼ tsp basil
- 1 cup mushrooms

DIRECTIONS

1. In a bowl combine all ingredients together and mix well
2. In a skillet heat olive oil and pour the egg mixture
3. Cook for 1-2 minutes per side
4. When ready remove omelette from the skillet and serve

BREAKFAST MIX

Serves: **1**

Prep Time: **5** Minutes

Cook Time: **5** Minutes

Total Time: **10** Minutes

INGREDIENTS

- 1 cup corn cereal
- 1 cup rice cereal
- ¼ cup cocoa cereal
- ¼ cup rice cakes

DIRECTIONS

1. In a bowl combine all ingredients together
2. Serve with milk

SAUSAGE BREAKFAST SANDWICH

Serves: 2
Prep Time: 5 Minutes
Cook Time: 15 Minutes
Total Time: 20 Minutes

INGREDIENTS

- ¼ cup egg substitute
- 1 muffin
- 1 turkey sausage patty
- 1 tablespoon cheddar cheese

DIRECTIONS

1. In a skillet pour egg and cook on low heat
2. Place turkey sausage patty in a pan and cook for 4-5 minutes per side
3. On a toasted muffin place the cooked egg, top with a sausage patty and cheddar cheese
4. Serve when ready

BREAKFAST GRANOLA

Serves: 2

Prep Time: 5 Minutes

Cook Time: 30 Minutes

Total Time: 35 Minutes

INGREDIENTS

- 1 tsp vanilla extract
- 1 tablespoon honey
- 1 lb. rolled oats
- 2 tablespoons sesame seeds
- ¼ lb. almonds
- ¼ lb. berries

DIRECTIONS

1. **Preheat the oven to 325 F**
2. **Spread the granola onto a baking sheet**
3. **Bake for 12-15 minutes, remove and mix everything**
4. **Bake for another 12-15 minutes or until slightly brown**
5. **When ready remove from the oven and serve**

PANCAKES

BANANA PANCAKES

Serves: **4**

Prep Time: **10** Minutes

Cook Time: **20** Minutes

Total Time: **30** Minutes

INGREDIENTS

- 1 cup whole wheat flour
- ¼ tsp baking soda
- ¼ tsp baking powder
- 1 cup mashed banana
- 2 eggs
- 1 cup milk

DIRECTIONS

1. In a bowl combine all ingredients together and mix well
2. In a skillet heat olive oil
3. Pour ¼ of the batter and cook each pancake for 1-2 minutes per side
4. When ready remove from heat and serve

PINEAPPLE PANCAKES

Serves: **4**

Prep Time: **10** Minutes

Cook Time: **20** Minutes

Total Time: **30** Minutes

INGREDIENTS

- 1 cup whole wheat flour
- ¼ tsp baking soda
- ¼ tsp baking powder
- 1 cup pineapple
- 2 eggs
- 1 cup milk

DIRECTIONS

1. In a bowl combine all ingredients together and mix well
2. In a skillet heat olive oil
3. Pour ¼ of the batter and cook each pancake for 1-2 minutes per side
4. When ready remove from heat and serve

ALMOND PANCAKES

Serves: **4**

Prep Time: **10** Minutes

Cook Time: **30** Minutes

Total Time: **40** Minutes

INGREDIENTS

- 1 cup whole wheat flour
- ¼ tsp baking soda
- ¼ tsp baking powder
- 1 cup almonds
- 2 eggs
- 1 cup milk

DIRECTIONS

1. In a bowl combine all ingredients together and mix well
2. In a skillet heat olive oil
3. Pour ¼ of the batter and cook each pancake for 1-2 minutes per side
4. When ready remove from heat and serve

APPLE PANCAKES

Serves: **4**

Prep Time: **10** Minutes

Cook Time: **20** Minutes

Total Time: **30** Minutes

INGREDIENTS

- 1 cup whole wheat flour
- ¼ tsp baking soda
- ¼ tsp baking powder
- 1 cup mashed apple
- 2 eggs
- 1 cup milk

DIRECTIONS

1. In a bowl combine all ingredients together and mix well
2. In a skillet heat olive oil
3. Pour ¼ of the batter and cook each pancake for 1-2 minutes per side
4. When ready remove from heat and serve

STRAWBERRY PANCAKES

Serves: **4**

Prep Time: **10** Minutes

Cook Time: **20** Minutes

Total Time: **30** Minutes

INGREDIENTS

- 1 cup whole wheat flour
- ¼ tsp baking soda
- ¼ tsp baking powder
- 1 cup strawberries
- 2 eggs
- 1 cup milk

DIRECTIONS

1. In a bowl combine all ingredients together and mix well
2. In a skillet heat olive oil
3. Pour ¼ of the batter and cook each pancake for 1-2 minutes per side
4. When ready remove from heat and serve

PEAR PANCAKES

Serves: **4**

Prep Time: **10** Minutes

Cook Time: **30** Minutes

Total Time: **40** Minutes

INGREDIENTS

- 1 cup whole wheat flour
- ¼ tsp baking soda
- ¼ tsp baking powder
- 2 eggs
- 1 cup milk
- 1 cup mashed pear

DIRECTIONS

1. In a bowl combine all ingredients together and mix well
2. In a skillet heat olive oil
3. Pour ¼ of the batter and cook each pancake for 1-2 minutes per side
4. When ready remove from heat and serve

COOKIES

BREAKFAST COOKIES

Serves: **8-12**

Prep Time: **5** Minutes

Cook Time: **15** Minutes

Total Time: **20** Minutes

INGREDIENTS

- 1 cup rolled oats
- ¼ cup applesauce
- ½ tsp vanilla extract
- 3 tablespoons chocolate chips
- 2 tablespoons dried fruits
- 1 tsp cinnamon

DIRECTIONS

1. Preheat the oven to 325 F
2. In a bowl combine all ingredients together and mix well
3. Scoop cookies using an ice cream scoop
4. Place cookies onto a prepared baking sheet
5. Place in the oven for 12-15 minutes or until the cookies are done
6. When ready remove from the oven and serve

SMOOOTHIES

FIG SMOOTHIE

Serves: **1**

Prep Time: **5** Minutes

Cook Time: **5** Minutes

Total Time: **10** Minutes

INGREDIENTS

- 1 cup ice
- 1 cup vanilla yogurt
- 1 cup coconut milk
- 1 tsp honey
- 4 figs

DIRECTIONS

1. In a blender place all ingredients and blend until smooth
2. Pour smoothie in a glass and serve

POMEGRANATE SMOOTHIE

Serves: *1*

Prep Time: *5* Minutes

Cook Time: *5* Minutes

Total Time: *10* Minutes

INGREDIENTS

- 2 cups blueberries
- 1 cup pomegranate
- 1 tablespoon honey
- 1 cup Greek yogurt

DIRECTIONS

1. In a blender place all ingredients and blend until smooth
2. Pour smoothie in a glass and serve

GINGER-KALE SMOOTHIE

Serves: **1**

Prep Time: **5** Minutes

Cook Time: **5** Minutes

Total Time: **10** Minutes

INGREDIENTS

- 1 cup kale
- 1 banana
- 1 cup almond milk
- 1 cup vanilla yogurt
- 1 tsp chia seeds
- ¼ tsp ginger

DIRECTIONS

1. **In a blender place all ingredients and blend until smooth**
2. **Pour smoothie in a glass and serve**

BERRY YOGHURT SMOOTHIE

Serves: *1*

Prep Time: *5* Minutes

Cook Time: *5* Minutes

Total Time: *10* Minutes

INGREDIENTS

- 6 oz. berries
- 2 bananas
- 4 oz. vanilla yoghurt
- 1 cup milk
- 1 tablespoon honey

DIRECTIONS

1. In a blender place all ingredients and blend until smooth
2. Pour smoothie in a glass and serve

COCONUT SMOOTHIE

Serves: **1**

Prep Time: **5** Minutes

Cook Time: **5** Minutes

Total Time: **10** Minutes

INGREDIENTS

- 2 mangoes
- 2 bananas
- 1 cup coconut water
- 1 cup ice
- 1 tablespoon honey
- 1 cup Greek Yoghurt
- 1 cup strawberries

DIRECTIONS

1. In a blender place all ingredients and blend until smooth
2. Pour smoothie in a glass and serve

RASPBERRY-VANILLA SMOOTHIE

Serves: **1**
Prep Time: **5** Minutes
Cook Time: **5** Minutes
Total Time: **10** Minutes

INGREDIENTS

- ¼ cup sugar
- ¼ cup water
- 1 cup Greek yoghurt
- 1 cup raspberries
- 1 tsp vanilla extract
- 1 cup ice

DIRECTIONS

1. In a blender place all ingredients and blend until smooth
2. Pour smoothie in a glass and serve

CHERRY SMOOTHIE

Serves: **1**

Prep Time: **5** Minutes

Cook Time: **5** Minutes

Total Time: **10** Minutes

INGREDIENTS

- 1 can cherries
- 2 tablespoons peanut butter
- 1 tablespoon honey
- 1 cup Greek Yoghurt
- 1 cup coconut milk

DIRECTIONS

1. **In a blender place all ingredients and blend until smooth**
2. **Pour smoothie in a glass and serve**

CHOCOLATE SMOOTHIE

Serves: **1**

Prep Time: **5** Minutes

Cook Time: **5** Minutes

Total Time: **10** Minutes

INGREDIENTS

- 2 bananas
- 1 cup Greek Yoghurt
- 1 tablespoon honey
- 1 tablespoon cocoa powder
- ½ cup chocolate chips
- ¼ cup almond milk

DIRECTIONS

1. In a blender place all ingredients and blend until smooth
2. Pour smoothie in a glass and serve

TOFU SMOOTHIE

Serves: **1**
Prep Time: **5** Minutes
Cook Time: **5** Minutes
Total Time: **10** Minutes

INGREDIENTS

- 1 cup blueberries
- ¼ cup tofu
- ¼ cup pomegranate juice
- 1 cup ice
- ½ cup agave nectar

DIRECTIONS

1. **In a blender place all ingredients and blend until smooth**
2. **Pour smoothie in a glass and serve**

ORANGE SMOOTHIE

Serves: **1**
Prep Time: **5** Minutes
Cook Time: **5** Minutes
Total Time: **10** Minutes

INGREDIENTS

- 1 orange
- ½ cup orange juice
- ½ banana
- 1 tsp vanilla essence

DIRECTIONS

1. In a blender place all ingredients and blend until smooth
2. Pour smoothie in a glass and serve

RAISIN DATE SMOOTHIE

Serves: **1**

Prep Time: **5** Minutes

Cook Time: **5** Minutes

Total Time: **10** Minutes

INGREDIENTS

- ¼ cup raisins
- 2 Medjool dates
- 1 cup berries
- 1 cup almond milk
- 1 tsp chia seeds

DIRECTIONS

1. **In a blender place all ingredients and blend until smooth**
2. **Pour smoothie in a glass and serve**

MUFFINS

SIMPLE MUFFINS

Serves: **8-12**
Prep Time: **10**   Minutes
Cook Time: **20**   Minutes
Total Time: **30**   Minutes

INGREDIENTS

- 2 eggs
- 1 tablespoon olive oil
- 1 cup milk
- 2 cups whole wheat flour
- 1 tsp baking soda
- ¼ tsp baking soda
- 1 cup pumpkin puree
- 1 tsp cinnamon
- ¼ cup molasses

DIRECTIONS

1. In a bowl combine all wet ingredients
2. In another bowl combine all dry ingredients
3. Combine wet and dry ingredients together
4. Pour mixture into 8-12 prepared muffin cups, fill 2/3 of the cups

5. Bake for 18-20 minutes at 375 F
6. When ready remove from the oven and serve

GINGERBREAD MUFFINS

Serves: *8-12*

Prep Time: *10* Minutes

Cook Time: *20* Minutes

Total Time: *30* Minutes

INGREDIENTS

- 2 eggs
- 1 tablespoon olive oil
- 1 cup milk
- 2 cups whole wheat flour
- 1 tsp baking soda
- ¼ tsp baking soda
- 1 tsp ginger
- 1 tsp cinnamon
- ¼ cup molasses

DIRECTIONS

1. In a bowl combine all wet ingredients
2. In another bowl combine all dry ingredients
3. Combine wet and dry ingredients together
4. Fold in ginger and mix well
5. Pour mixture into 8-12 prepared muffin cups, fill 2/3 of the cups

6. Bake for 18-20 minutes at 375 F
7. When ready remove from the oven and serve

CHERRIES MUFFINS

Serves: **8-12**
Prep Time: **10** Minutes
Cook Time: **20** Minutes
Total Time: **30** Minutes

INGREDIENTS

- 2 eggs
- 1 tablespoon olive oil
- 1 cup milk
- 2 cups whole wheat flour
- 1 tsp baking soda
- ¼ tsp baking soda
- 1 tsp cinnamon
- 1 cup mashed cherries

DIRECTIONS

1. In a bowl combine all wet ingredients
2. In another bowl combine all dry ingredients
3. Combine wet and dry ingredients together
4. Pour mixture into 8-12 prepared muffin cups, fill 2/3 of the cups
5. Bake for 18-20 minutes at 375 F
6. When ready remove from the oven and serve

BLUEBERRY MUFFINS

Serves: **8-12**
Prep Time: **10** Minutes
Cook Time: **20** Minutes
Total Time: **30** Minutes

INGREDIENTS

- 2 eggs
- 1 tablespoon olive oil
- 1 cup milk
- 2 cups whole wheat flour
- 1 tsp baking soda
- ¼ tsp baking soda
- 1 tsp cinnamon
- 1 cup blueberries

DIRECTIONS

1. In a bowl combine all wet ingredients
2. In another bowl combine all dry ingredients
3. Combine wet and dry ingredients together
4. Fold in blueberries and mix well
5. Pour mixture into 8-12 prepared muffin cups, fill 2/3 of the cups
6. Bake for 18-20 minutes at 375 F

BERRIES MUFFINS

Serves: **8-12**

Prep Time: **10** Minutes

Cook Time: **20** Minutes

Total Time: **30** Minutes

INGREDIENTS

- 2 eggs
- 1 tablespoon olive oil
- 1 cup milk
- 2 cups whole wheat flour
- 1 tsp baking soda
- ¼ tsp baking soda
- 1 tsp cinnamon
- 1 cup berries

DIRECTIONS

1. In a bowl combine all wet ingredients
2. In another bowl combine all dry ingredients
3. Combine wet and dry ingredients together
4. Pour mixture into 8-12 prepared muffin cups, fill 2/3 of the cups
5. Bake for 18-20 minutes at 375 F
6. When ready remove from the oven and serve

CHOCOLATE MUFFINS

Serves: **8-12**

Prep Time: **10** Minutes

Cook Time: **20** Minutes

Total Time: **30** Minutes

INGREDIENTS

- 2 eggs
- 1 tablespoon olive oil
- 1 cup milk
- 2 cups whole wheat flour
- 1 tsp baking soda
- ¼ tsp baking soda
- 1 tsp cinnamon
- 1 cup chocolate chips

DIRECTIONS

1. In a bowl combine all wet ingredients
2. In another bowl combine all dry ingredients
3. Combine wet and dry ingredients together
4. Fold in chocolate chips and mix well
5. Pour mixture into 8-12 prepared muffin cups, fill 2/3 of the cups
6. Bake for 18-20 minutes at 375 F

RASPBERRIES MUFFINS

Serves: **8-12**

Prep Time: **10** Minutes

Cook Time: **20** Minutes

Total Time: **30** Minutes

INGREDIENTS

- 2 eggs
- 1 tablespoon olive oil
- 1 cup milk
- 2 cups whole wheat flour
- 1 tsp baking soda
- ¼ tsp baking soda
- 1 tsp cinnamon
- 1 cup raspberries

DIRECTIONS

1. In a bowl combine all wet ingredients
2. In another bowl combine all dry ingredients
3. Combine wet and dry ingredients together
4. Pour mixture into 8-12 prepared muffin cups, fill 2/3 of the cups
5. Bake for 18-20 minutes at 375 F
6. When ready remove from the oven and serve

SECOND COOKBOOK

BREAKFAST RECIPES

PANCAKES

Serves: **4**

Prep Time: **10** Minutes

Cook Time: **10** Minutes

Total Time: **20** Minutes

INGREDIENTS

- 1 cup millet flour
- ½ cup soy flour
- 1 tablespoon baking powder
- ¼ tsp salt
- 1 egg
- 1 cup water
- 2 tablespoons oil

DIRECTIONS

1. In a bowl mix all dry ingredients
2. Stir together all liquids and add to dry ingredients
3. Bake on griddle for 1-2 minutes per side
4. Remove and serve

BLUEBERRY PANCAKES

Serves: **4**

Prep Time: **10** Minutes

Cook Time: **20** Minutes

Total Time: **30** Minutes

INGREDIENTS

- 1 cup whole wheat flour
- ¼ tsp baking soda
- ¼ tsp baking powder
- 1 cup blueberries
- 2 eggs
- 1 cup milk

DIRECTIONS

1. In a bowl combine all ingredients together and mix well
2. In a skillet heat olive oil
3. Pour ¼ of the batter and cook each pancake for 1-2 minutes per side
4. When ready remove from heat and serve

ALMOND PANCAKES

Serves: **4**

Prep Time: **10** Minutes

Cook Time: **30** Minutes

Total Time: **40** Minutes

INGREDIENTS

- 1 cup whole wheat flour
- ¼ tsp baking soda
- ¼ tsp baking powder
- 1 cup almonds
- 2 eggs
- 1 cup milk

DIRECTIONS

1. In a bowl combine all ingredients together and mix well
2. In a skillet heat olive oil
3. Pour ¼ of the batter and cook each pancake for 1-2 minutes per side
4. When ready remove from heat and serve

BANANA PANCAKES

Serves: **4**

Prep Time: **10** Minutes

Cook Time: **20** Minutes

Total Time: **30** Minutes

INGREDIENTS

- 1 cup whole wheat flour
- ¼ tsp baking soda
- ¼ tsp baking powder
- 1 cup mashed banana
- 2 eggs
- 1 cup milk

DIRECTIONS

1. In a bowl combine all ingredients together and mix well
2. In a skillet heat olive oil
3. Pour ¼ of the batter and cook each pancake for 1-2 minutes per side
4. When ready remove from heat and serve

STRAWBERRY PANCAKES

Serves: **4**

Prep Time: **10** Minutes

Cook Time: **20** Minutes

Total Time: **30** Minutes

INGREDIENTS

- 1 cup whole wheat flour
- ¼ tsp baking soda
- ¼ tsp baking powder
- 1 cup strawberries
- 2 eggs
- 1 cup milk

DIRECTIONS

1. **In a bowl combine all ingredients together and mix well**
2. **In a skillet heat olive oil**
3. **Pour ¼ of the batter and cook each pancake for 1-2 minutes per side**
4. **When ready remove from heat and serve**

SIMPLE PANCAKES

Serves: **4**

Prep Time: **10** Minutes

Cook Time: **30** Minutes

Total Time: **40** Minutes

INGREDIENTS

- 1 cup whole wheat flour
- ¼ tsp baking soda
- ¼ tsp baking powder
- 2 eggs
- 1 cup milk

DIRECTIONS

1. In a bowl combine all ingredients together and mix well
2. In a skillet heat olive oil
3. Pour ¼ of the batter and cook each pancake for 1-2 minutes per side
4. When ready remove from heat and serve

GINGERBREAD MUFFINS

Serves: **8-12**

Prep Time: **10** Minutes

Cook Time: **20** Minutes

Total Time: **30** Minutes

INGREDIENTS

- 2 eggs
- 1 tablespoon olive oil
- 1 cup milk
- 2 cups whole wheat flour
- 1 tsp baking soda
- ¼ tsp baking soda
- 1 tsp ginger
- 1 tsp cinnamon
- ¼ cup molasses

DIRECTIONS

1. In a bowl combine all dry ingredients
2. In another bowl combine all dry ingredients
3. Combine wet and dry ingredients together
4. Fold in ginger and mix well
5. Pour mixture into 8-12 prepared muffin cups, fill 2/3 of the cups

6. Bake for 18-20 minutes at 375 F
7. When ready remove from the oven and serve

BANANA MUFFINS

Serves: **8-12**
Prep Time: **10**   Minutes
Cook Time: **20**   Minutes
Total Time: **30**   Minutes

INGREDIENTS

- 2 eggs
- 1 tablespoon olive oil
- 1 cup milk
- 2 cups whole wheat flour
- 1 tsp baking soda
- ¼ tsp baking soda
- 1 tsp cinnamon
- 1 cup mashed banana

DIRECTIONS

1. In a bowl combine all dry ingredients
2. In another bowl combine all dry ingredients
3. Combine wet and dry ingredients together
4. Fold in mashed banana and mix well
5. Pour mixture into 8-12 prepared muffin cups, fill 2/3 of the cups
6. Bake for 18-20 minutes at 375 F, when ready remove and serve

BLUEBERRY MUFFINS

Serves: **8-12**

Prep Time: **10** Minutes

Cook Time: **20** Minutes

Total Time: **30** Minutes

INGREDIENTS

- 2 eggs
- 1 tablespoon olive oil
- 1 cup milk
- 2 cups whole wheat flour
- 1 tsp baking soda
- ¼ tsp baking soda
- 1 tsp cinnamon
- 1 cup blueberries

DIRECTIONS

1. In a bowl combine all dry ingredients
2. In another bowl combine all dry ingredients
3. Combine wet and dry ingredients together
4. Fold in blueberries and mix well
5. Pour mixture into 8-12 prepared muffin cups, fill 2/3 of the cups
6. Bake for 18-20 minutes at 375 F, when ready remove and serve

STRAWBERRY MUFFINS

Serves: *8-12*
Prep Time: *10*   Minutes
Cook Time: *20*   Minutes
Total Time: *30*   Minutes

INGREDIENTS

- 2 eggs
- 1 tablespoon olive oil
- 1 cup milk
- 2 cups whole wheat flour
- 1 tsp baking soda
- ¼ tsp baking soda
- 1 tsp cinnamon
- 1 cup strawberries

DIRECTIONS

1. In a bowl combine all dry ingredients
2. In another bowl combine all dry ingredients
3. Combine wet and dry ingredients together
4. Fold in strawberries and mix well
5. Pour mixture into 8-12 prepared muffin cups, fill 2/3 of the cups
6. Bake for 18-20 minutes at 375 F, when ready remove and serve

CHOCOLATE MUFFINS

Serves: **8-12**

Prep Time: **10** Minutes

Cook Time: **20** Minutes

Total Time: **30** Minutes

INGREDIENTS

- 2 eggs
- 1 tablespoon olive oil
- 1 cup milk
- 2 cups whole wheat flour
- 1 tsp baking soda
- ¼ tsp baking soda
- 1 tsp cinnamon
- 1 cup chocolate chips

DIRECTIONS

1. In a bowl combine all dry ingredients
2. In another bowl combine all dry ingredients
3. Combine wet and dry ingredients together
4. Fold in chocolate chips and mix well
5. Pour mixture into 8-12 prepared muffin cups, fill 2/3 of the cups
6. Bake for 18-20 minutes at 375 F, when ready remove and serve

SIMPLE MUFFINS

Serves: **8-12**

Prep Time: **10** Minutes

Cook Time: **20** Minutes

Total Time: **30** Minutes

INGREDIENTS

- 2 eggs
- 1 tablespoon olive oil
- 1 cup milk
- 2 cups whole wheat flour
- 1 tsp baking soda
- ¼ tsp baking soda
- 1 tsp cinnamon

DIRECTIONS

1. In a bowl combine all dry ingredients
2. In another bowl combine all dry ingredients
3. Combine wet and dry ingredients together
4. Pour mixture into 8-12 prepared muffin cups, fill 2/3 of the cups
5. Bake for 18-20 minutes at 375 F
6. When ready remove from the oven and serve

BERRY FRENCH TOAST

Serves: 2

Prep Time: 10 Minutes

Cook Time: 15 Minutes

Total Time: 25 Minutes

INGREDIENTS

- 2 bread slices
- 1tsp lemon juice
- 1 tsp vanilla extract
- 2 eggs
- ¼ cup heavy cream
- 1 tsp cinnamon
- ¼ cup maple syrup
- 1 cup blueberries

DIRECTIONS

1. In a bowl combine all ingredients for the dipping
2. Dip the bread slices in the mixture and let them soak for 2-3 minutes
3. When ready fry the bread for 2-3 minutes per side
4. When ready remove from the skillet and serve with blueberries and maple syrup

POHA WAFFLES

Serves: **4**

Prep Time: **10** Minutes

Cook Time: **10** Minutes

Total Time: **20** Minutes

INGREDIENTS

- ½ cup rice flour
- 1 tsp baking soda
- 1 banana
- ½ tsp salt
- 2 tablespoons oil
- ½ cup milk
- 1 tsp cider vinegar
- 1 egg
- ½ cup quinoa flakes
- 1 tablespoon honey

DIRECTIONS

1. In a bowl mix all dry ingredients
2. Separate egg yolk from egg white and beet egg white
3. Mix egg yolk with milk, honey, wet fruit and add dry ingredients to mixture
4. Add cider vinegar and mix gently

5. Pour mixture into waffle iron
6. When remove and serve

BREAKFAST BISCUITS

Serves: **12**

Prep Time: **10** Minutes

Cook Time: **15** Minutes

Total Time: **25** Minutes

INGREDIENTS

- 2 cups flour
- 1 tsp xantham gum
- ½ tsp salt
- 4 tablespoons margarine
- ¾ cup vance's darifree
- 1 tablespoon baking powder
- 1 tsp sugar

DIRECTIONS

1. Preheat oven to 425 F
2. Toss together all ingredients, gather into a ball
3. Form small biscuits and bake for 12-15 minutes
4. Remove and serve

INDIAN PANCAKES

Serves: **2**

Prep Time: **10** Minutes

Cook Time: **10** Minutes

Total Time: **20** Minutes

INGREDIENTS

- 1 cup chick pea flour
- 1 tablespoon ginger
- 1/3 cup chopped green onions
- 1 cu water

DIRECTIONS

1. In a bowl whisk all ingredients together
2. Pour mixture in a pan and cook 1-2 minutes per side
3. Remove and serve with honey

COOKED MILLET

Serves: **4**

Prep Time: **10** Minutes

Cook Time: **20** Minutes

Total Time: **30** Minutes

INGREDIENTS

- 1 cup millet grains
- 3 cups water

DIRECTIONS

1. In a pot toast 1 cup of millet grains until golden brown
2. Add water and bring to boil, stir constantly
3. Cook on low heat for 20 minutes
4. Remove and serve

MUFFIN MIX

Serves: **10**

Prep Time: **10** Minutes

Cook Time: **20** Minutes

Total Time: **30** Minutes

INGREDIENTS

- ¼ cup sugar
- ¼ tsp salt
- ¼ tsp vanilla
- 2 tablespoons shortening
- 1 tablespoon baking powder
- ½ cup milk
- 2 eggs
- 1 cup GF flour mix

DIRECTIONS

1. In a bowl mix together shortening with sugar
2. Sift together the flour, milk, baking powder, salt and beaten eggs
3. Stir in vanilla and pour muffin mixture into muffin cups
4. Bake at 325 F for 15-20 minutes
5. Remove and serve

BANANA BREAD

Serves: **4**

Prep Time: **10** Minutes

Cook Time: **60** Minutes

Total Time: **70** Minutes

INGREDIENTS

- 1 cup soy flour
- 1 ½ tsp baking powder
- ½ tsp xanthan gum
- ½ tsp salt
- ½ cup mashed banana
- 2/4 tsp baking soda
- ½ cup shortening
- ½ cup potato starch flour
- ½ cup rice flour
- 2/3 up honey
- 2 eggs beaten

DIRECTIONS

1. In a bowl mix all dry ingredients together
2. Mix honey and shortening until light and fluffy and add beaten eggs

3. Add dry ingredients with the mashed banana and mix until smooth
4. Pour mixture into a loaf pan and bake for 60 minutes at 325 F

FRITTER

Serves: **4**

Prep Time: **10** Minutes

Cook Time: **20** Minutes

Total Time: **30** Minutes

INGREDIENTS

- 2 cornstarch
- 2 tablespoons rice flour
- 2 packs rise yeast
- 1 egg
- cornstarch bread
- 5 tablespoons potato starch
- 2 tablespoons almonds
- 2 cups water
- 2 tablespoons oil
- 1 tsp salt
- ¼ cup sugar
- 1 tsp xanthan gum

DIRECTIONS

1. **In a bowl combine all dry ingredients**
2. **Add hot water to mixture and beat with a mixer for 4-5 minutes**

3. Add oil and beat again for 2-3 minutes
4. Cook until golden brown, remove and serve

HOT CHOCOLATE MIX

Serves: **4**

Prep Time: **10** Minutes

Cook Time: **30** Minutes

Total Time: **40** Minutes

INGREDIENTS

- 4 cups dari-free
- 1 cup sugar
- ¼ tsp salt
- ¾ cup cocoa powder

DIRECTIONS

1. In a bowl mix all ingredients
2. Place 4 tablespoons mix in a cup
3. Add boiling water and stir to dissolve mix

PANCAKE SYRUP

Serves: **4**

Prep Time: **10** Minutes

Cook Time: **30** Minutes

Total Time: **40** Minutes

INGREDIENTS

- 3 cups corn syrup
- 1 cup maple syrup

DIRECTIONS

1. In a jar mix maple syrup with corn syrup
2. 100% pure ingredients are required for this GFCF recipe

PINEAPPLE BREAKFAST CAKE

Serves: **4**
Prep Time: **10** Minutes

Cook Time: **40** Minutes

Total Time: **50** Minutes

INGREDIENTS

- 3 eggs
- 1 tablespoon cinnamon
- 18-ounce can pineapple
- 1 tsp baking soda
- 1 tsp GF vanilla
- 4 ounces GF bread
- ½ cup sugar

DIRECTIONS

1. In a blender add crushed pineapple and the rest of the ingredients, blend until smooth
2. Pour mixture into a pan and sprinkle with cinnamon
3. Bake at 325 F for 40 minutes

SCRAMBLED EGGS WITH RICE

Serves: **4**

Prep Time: **10** Minutes

Cook Time: **10** Minutes

Total Time: **20** Minutes

INGREDIENTS

- ¼ cup onion
- ¼ cup margarine
- 4 eggs
- 1/3 cup rice
- ½ tsp salt
- 1 cup grated cheese

DIRECTIONS

1. In a pot cook margarine and onion until golden brown
2. In a bowl mix milk and eggs, add rice, cheese and salt
3. Pour mixture over onion and cook or 4-5 minutes
4. Remove and serve

TART RECIPES

APPLE TART

Serves: **6-8**

Prep Time: **25** Minutes

Cook Time: **25** Minutes

Total Time: **50** Minutes

INGREDIENTS

- pastry sheets

FILLING
- 1 tsp lemon juice
- 3 oz. brown sugar
- 1 lb. apples
- 150 ml double cream
- 2 eggs

DIRECTIONS

1. Preheat oven to 400 F, unfold pastry sheets and place them on a baking sheet
2. Toss together all ingredients together and mix well
3. Spread mixture in a single layer on the pastry sheets
4. Before baking decorate with your desired fruits
5. Bake at 400 F for 22-25 minutes or until golden brown

6. When ready remove from the oven and serve

CHOCHOLATE TART

Serves: **6-8**

Prep Time: **25** Minutes

Cook Time: **25** Minutes

Total Time: **50** Minutes

INGREDIENTS

- pastry sheets
- 1 tsp vanilla extract
- ½ lb. caramel
- ½ lb. black chocolate
- 4-5 tablespoons butter
- 3 eggs
- ¼ lb. brown sugar

DIRECTIONS

1. Preheat oven to 400 F, unfold pastry sheets and place them on a baking sheet
2. Toss together all ingredients together and mix well
3. Spread mixture in a single layer on the pastry sheets
4. Before baking decorate with your desired fruits
5. Bake at 400 F for 22-25 minutes or until golden brown
6. When ready remove from the oven and serve

PIE RECIPES

PEACH PECAN PIE

Serves: **8-12**

Prep Time: **15** Minutes
Cook Time: **35** Minutes
Total Time: **50** Minutes

INGREDIENTS

- 4-5 cups peaches
- 1 tablespoon preserves
- 1 cup sugar
- 4 small egg yolks
- ¼ cup flour
- 1 tsp vanilla extract

DIRECTIONS

1. Line a pie plate or pie form with pastry and cover the edges of the plate depending on your preference
2. In a bowl combine all pie ingredients together and mix well
3. Pour the mixture over the pastry
4. Bake at 400-425 F for 25-30 minutes or until golden brown
5. When ready remove from the oven and let it rest for 15 minutes

BLUEBERRY PIE

Serves: **8-12**

Prep Time: **15** Minutes

Cook Time: **35** Minutes

Total Time: **50** Minutes

INGREDIENTS

- pastry sheets
- ¼ tsp lavender
- 1 cup brown sugar
- 4-5 cups blueberries
- 1 tablespoon lemon juice
- 1 cup almonds
- 2 tablespoons butter

DIRECTIONS

1. Line a pie plate or pie form with pastry and cover the edges of the plate depending on your preference
2. In a bowl combine all pie ingredients together and mix well
3. Pour the mixture over the pastry
4. Bake at 400-425 F for 25-30 minutes or until golden brown
5. When ready remove from the oven and let it rest for 15 minutes

PUMPKIN PIE

Serves: *8-12*
Prep Time: *15* Minutes
Cook Time: *35* Minutes
Total Time: *50* Minutes

INGREDIENTS

- pastry sheets
- 1 cup buttermilk
- 1 can pumpkin
- 1 cup sugar
- 1 tsp cinnamon
- 1 tsp vanilla extract
- 2 eggs

DIRECTIONS

1. Line a pie plate or pie form with pastry and cover the edges of the plate depending on your preference
2. In a bowl combine all pie ingredients together and mix well
3. Pour the mixture over the pastry
4. Bake at 400-425 F for 25-30 minutes or until golden brown
5. When ready remove from the oven and let it rest for 15 minutes

SMOOTHIE RECIPES

GREEN SMOOTHIE

Serves: **1**

Prep Time: **5** Minutes

Cook Time: **5** Minutes

Total Time: **10** Minutes

INGREDIENTS

- 1 banana
- 1 cup pineapple chunks
- 1 cup mango chunks
- 1 cup kale
- 1 cup ice
- ½ cup almond milk

DIRECTIONS

1. In a blender place all ingredients and blend until smooth
2. Pour smoothie in a glass and serve

WAKE UP SMOOTHIE

Serves: **1**

Prep Time: **5** Minutes

Cook Time: **5** Minutes

Total Time: **10** Minutes

INGREDIENTS

- 1 banana
- 1 cup coffee
- ¼ cup milk
- 1 pinch cinnamon
-

DIRECTIONS

1. In a blender place all ingredients and blend until smooth
2. Pour smoothie in a glass and serve

RASPBERRY SMOOTHIE

Serves: *1*
Prep Time: *5* Minutes
Cook Time: *5* Minutes
Total Time: *10* Minutes

INGREDIENTS

- 1 cup raspberries
- ½ cup coconut milk
- 1 cup mango
- ¼ cup pear juice

DIRECTIONS

1. In a blender place all ingredients and blend until smooth
2. Pour smoothie in a glass and serve

CHOCOLATE SMOOTHIE

Serves: *1*

Prep Time: *5* Minutes

Cook Time: *5* Minutes

Total Time: *10* Minutes

INGREDIENTS

- 1 banana
- 1 tsp cocoa powder
- 1 cup almond milk
- 1 cup chocolate chips

DIRECTIONS

1. In a blender place all ingredients and blend until smooth
2. Pour smoothie in a glass and serve

PROTEIN SMOOTHIE

Serves: *1*
Prep Time: *5* Minutes

Cook Time: *5* Minutes

Total Time: *10* Minutes

INGREDIENTS

- ¼ avocado
- ¼ cup Greek Yogurt
- 1 tablespoon honey
- 1 cup low-fat milk
- 1 cup ice
- ¼ cup spinach

DIRECTIONS

1. **In a blender place all ingredients and blend until smooth**
2. **Pour smoothie in a glass and serve**

SUNSHINE SMOOTHIE

Serves: **1**

Prep Time: **5** Minutes

Cook Time: **5** Minutes

Total Time: **10** Minutes

INGREDIENTS

- 1 banana
- 1 cup almond milk
- Juice from 1 orange
- 1 tablespoon goji berries
- 1 cup ice

DIRECTIONS

1. In a blender place all ingredients and blend until smooth
2. Pour smoothie in a glass and serve

MANGO SMOOTHIE

Serves: **1**

Prep Time: **5** Minutes

Cook Time: **5** Minutes

Total Time: **10** Minutes

INGREDIENTS

- 1 cup mango
- 1 cup spinach
- ¼ avocado
- 1 cup milk
- 1 tsp vanilla extract

DIRECTIONS

1. In a blender place all ingredients and blend until smooth
2. Pour smoothie in a glass and serve

PEACH SMOOTHIE

Serves: **1**

Prep Time: **5** Minutes

Cook Time: **5** Minutes

Total Time: **10** Minutes

INGREDIENTS

- 1 cup almond milk
- 2 peaches
- 1 banana
- 1 cup ice
- 1 tablespoon honey
- 1 tsp almond extract

DIRECTIONS

1. **In a blender place all ingredients and blend until smooth**
2. **Pour smoothie in a glass and serve**

PUMPKIN SMOOTHIE

Serves: **1**
Prep Time: **5** Minutes
Cook Time: **5** Minutes
Total Time: **10** Minutes

INGREDIENTS

- ¼ cup oats
- ½ cup puree
- 4 oz. Greek Yogurt
- 1 apple
- ½ cup almond milk
- 1 cup ice

DIRECTIONS

1. In a blender place all ingredients and blend until smooth
2. Pour smoothie in a glass and serve

ICE-CREAM RECIPES

COFFE ICE-CREAM

Serves: **6-8**

Prep Time: **15** Minutes
Cook Time: **15** Minutes
Total Time: **30** Minutes

INGREDIENTS

- 4 egg yolks
- 1 cup black coffee
- 2 cups heavy cream
- 1 cup half-and-half
- 1 cup brown sugar
- 1 tsp vanilla extract

DIRECTIONS

1. In a saucepan whisk together all ingredients
2. Mix until bubbly
3. Strain into a bowl and cool
4. Whisk in favorite fruits and mix well
5. Cover and refrigerate for 2-3 hours
6. Pour mixture in the ice-cream maker and follow manufacturer instructions

STRAWBERRY ICE-CREAM

Serves: **6-8**

Prep Time: **15** Minutes
Cook Time: **15** Minutes
Total Time: **30** Minutes

INGREDIENTS

- 1 lb. strawberries
- ½ cup sugar
- 1 tablespoon vanilla extract
- 1 cup heavy cram
- 1-pint vanilla

DIRECTIONS

1. In a saucepan whisk together all ingredients
2. Mix until bubbly
3. Strain into a bowl and cool
4. Whisk in favorite fruits and mix well
5. Cover and refrigerate for 2-3 hours
6. Pour mixture in the ice-cream maker and follow manufacturer instructions
7. Serve when ready

THIRD COOKBOOK

SIDE DISHES

FRIED VEGETABLES

Serves: 2

Prep Time: 10 Minutes

Cook Time: 15 Minutes

Total Time: 25 Minutes

INGREDIENTS

- 1 cup red bell pepper
- ¼ cup cucumber
- ¼ cup zucchini
- ¼ cup asparagus
- ¼ cup carrots
- 1 onion
- 2 eggs
- 1 tsp salt
- 1 tsp pepper
- Seasoning
- 1 tablespoon olive oil

DIRECTIONS

1. In a skillet heat olive oil and sauté onion until soft
2. Chop vegetables into thin slices and pour over onion

3. Whisk eggs with salt and pepper and pour over the vegetables
4. Cook until vegetables are brown
5. When ready remove from heat and serve

ONION SAUCE

Serves: **4**

Prep Time: **10** Minutes

Cook Time: **55** Minutes

Total Time: **65** Minutes

INGREDIENTS

- 1 onion
- 2 garlic cloves
- ¼ lb. carrots
- 1 potato
- 1 tablespoon balsamic vinegar
- ¼ tsp salt
- ¼ tsp black pepper
- 1 tablespoon olive oil
- 1 cup water

DIRECTIONS

1. Chop all the vegetables and place them in a heated skillet
2. Add remaining ingredients and cook on low heat
3. Allow to simmer for 40-45 minutes or until vegetables are soft
4. Transfer mixture to a blender and blend until smooth
5. When ready remove from the blender and serve

FISH "CAKE"

Serves: **4-6**

Prep Time: **10** Minutes

Cook Time: **50** Minutes

Total Time: **60** Minutes

INGREDIENTS

- 2 tuna tins
- 2 potatoes
- 2 eggs
- 1 handful of gluten free flour
- 1 handful of parsley
- black pepper
- 1 cup breadcrumbs

DIRECTIONS

1. Preheat the oven to 350 F
2. Boil the potatoes until they are soft
3. Mix the tuna with parsley, black pepper and salt
4. Roll fish into patties and dip into a bowl with flour, then eggs and then breadcrumbs
5. Place the patties on a baking tray
6. Bake at 350 F for 40-45 minutes
7. When ready remove from heat and serve

SUSHI HANDROLLS

Serves: 2

Prep Time: 10 Minutes

Cook Time: 25 Minutes

Total Time: 35 Minutes

INGREDIENTS

- 1 sushi nori packet
- 4 tablespoons mayonnaise
- ½ lb. smoked salmon
- 1 tsp wasabi
- 1 cup cooked sushi rice
- 1 avocado

DIRECTIONS

1. Cut avocado and into thin slices
2. Take a sheet of sushi and spread mayonnaise onto the sheet
3. Add rice, salmon and avocado
4. Roll and dip sushi into wasabi and serve

STEAMED VEGETABLES

Serves: **2**

Prep Time: **10** Minutes

Cook Time: **10** Minutes

Total Time: **20** Minutes

INGREDIENTS

- 1 carrot
- 2 sweet potato
- 2 parsnips
- 1 zucchini
- 2 broccoli stems

DIRECTIONS

1. Chop vegetables into thin slices
2. Place all the vegetables into a steamer
3. Add enough water and cook on high until vegetables are steamed
4. When ready remove from the steamer and serve

GUACAMOLE

Serves: 2

Prep Time: 5 Minutes

Cook Time: 5 Minutes

Total Time: 10 Minutes

INGREDIENTS

- 1 avocado
- 1 lime juice
- 1 handful of coriander
- 1 tsp olive oil
- 1 tsp salt
- 1 tsp pepper

DIRECTIONS

1. Place all the ingredients in a blender
2. Blend until smooth and transfer to a bowl

CHICKEN NACHOS

Serves: **4-6**

Prep Time: **15** Minutes

Cook Time: **35** Minutes

Total Time: **50** Minutes

INGREDIENTS

- 2 chicken breasts
- Tortilla chips
- Fajita seasoning
- ¼ cup cheddar cheese
- 4-5 mushrooms
- Guacamole
- ¼ cup peppers

DIRECTIONS

1. In a pan heat olive oil and add chopped onion, sauté until soft
2. Add chicken, fajita seasoning and remaining vegetables
3. Cook on low heat for 10-12 minutes
4. Place tortilla chips into a baking dish, sprinkle cheese and bake in the oven until cheese has melted
5. Remove from the oven pour sautéed vegetables and chicken over and tortilla chips and serve

SCRAMBLED EGGS WITH SALMON

Serves: **2**

Prep Time: **10** Minutes

Cook Time: **20** Minutes

Total Time: **30** Minutes

INGREDIENTS

- ½ lb. smoked salmon
- 2 eggs
- 1 avocado
- 1 tsp salt
- 1 tsp pepper
- 1 tps olive oil

DIRECTIONS

1. In a bowl whisk the eggs with salt and pepper
2. In a skillet heat olive oil and pour the egg mixture
3. Add salmon pieces to the mixture and cook for 2-3 minutes per side
4. When ready remove from the skillet, add avocado and serve

CHICKEN WITH RICE

Serves: **4**

Prep Time: **10** Minutes

Cook Time: **25** Minutes

Total Time: **35** Minutes

INGREDIENTS

- 2 chicken breasts
- 1 cup cooked white rice
- 2 tablespoons mayonnaise
- 1 tablespoon curry powder
- 1 zucchini
- 1 cup broccoli
- 1 tablespoon olive oil

DIRECTIONS

1. Cut chicken breast into small pieces and set aside
2. In a pan heat olive oil and cook the chicken breast for 4-5 minutes
3. In another bowl combine mayonnaise, curry powder and add mixture to the chicken
4. Add remaining ingredients and cook for another 10-12 minutes or until the chicken is ready
5. When ready remove from the pot and serve with white rice

ROASTED VEGETABLES

Serves: **2**

Prep Time: **10** Minutes

Cook Time: **50** Minutes

Total Time: **60** Minutes

INGREDIENTS

- 1 carrot
- 2 sweet potatoes
- 1 butternut squash
- 2 parsnips
- 1 rosemary spring
- 2 bay leaves

DIRECTIONS

1. Chop the vegetables into thin slices
2. Place everything in a prepare baking dish
3. Bake at 350 F for 40-45 minutes or until vegetables are golden brown
4. When ready remove from the oven and serve

SAUSAGE PIZZA

Serves: **6-8**

Prep Time: **10** Minutes

Cook Time: **15** Minutes

Total Time: **25** Minutes

INGREDIENTS

- 2 pork sausages
- 1 tablespoon olive oil
- 2 garlic cloves
- 1 tsp fennel seeds
- ½ lb. ricotta
- 1 cup mozzarella cheese
- 1 oz. parmesan cheese
- 1 pizza crust

DIRECTIONS

1. Spread tomato sauce on the pizza crust
2. Place all the toppings on the pizza crust
3. Bake the pizza at 425 F for 12-15 minutes
4. When ready remove pizza from the oven and serve

HEALTY PIZZA

Serves: **6-8**

Prep Time: **10** Minutes

Cook Time: **15** Minutes

Total Time: **25** Minutes

INGREDIENTS

- 1 pizza crust
- 1 tablespoon olive oil
- 1 garlic clove
- 1 cup tomatoes
- 1 cup mozzarella cheese
- 1 carrot
- 1 cucumber

DIRECTIONS

1. Spread tomato sauce on the pizza crust
2. Place all the toppings on the pizza crust
3. Bake the pizza at 425 F for 12-15 minutes
4. When ready remove pizza from the oven and serve

SLAW

Serves: **1**
Prep Time: **5** Minutes
Cook Time: **5** Minutes
Total Time: **10** Minutes

INGREDIENTS

- 1 cabbage
- 1 bunch of baby carrots
- ½ cucumber
- 1 bun of cilantro
- 1 bunch of basil
- 1 onion

DIRECTIONS

1. **In a bowl combine all ingredients together and mix well**
2. **Serve with dressing**

EDAMAME FRITATTA

Serves: 2
Prep Time: 10 Minutes
Cook Time: 20 Minutes
Total Time: 30 Minutes

INGREDIENTS

- 1 cup edamame
- 1 tablespoon olive oil
- ½ red onion
- 2 eggs
- ¼ tsp salt
- 2 oz. cheddar cheese
- 1 garlic clove
- ¼ tsp dill

DIRECTIONS

1. In a bowl whisk eggs with salt and cheese
2. In a frying pan heat olive oil and pour egg mixture
3. Add remaining ingredients and mix well
4. Serve when ready

ONION FRITATTA

Serves: **2**

Prep Time: **10** Minutes

Cook Time: **20** Minutes

Total Time: **30** Minutes

INGREDIENTS

- 1 tablespoon olive oil
- ½ red onion
- 2 eggs
- ¼ tsp salt
- 2 oz. cheddar cheese
- 1 garlic clove
- ¼ tsp dill

DIRECTIONS

1. In a bowl whisk eggs with salt and cheese
2. In a frying pan heat olive oil and pour egg mixture
3. Add remaining ingredients and mix well
4. Serve when ready

LEAF FRITATTA

Serves: 2

Prep Time: 10 Minutes

Cook Time: 20 Minutes

Total Time: 30 Minutes

INGREDIENTS

- ½ lb. leaf
- 1 tablespoon olive oil
- ½ red onion
- 2 eggs
- ¼ tsp salt
- 2 oz. cheddar cheese
- 1 garlic clove
- ¼ tsp dill

DIRECTIONS

1. In a bowl whisk eggs with salt and cheese
2. In a frying pan heat olive oil and pour egg mixture
3. Add remaining ingredients and mix well
4. Serve when ready

KALE FRITATTA

Serves: **2**

Prep Time: **10** Minutes

Cook Time: **20** Minutes

Total Time: **30** Minutes

INGREDIENTS

- 1 cup kale
- 1 tablespoon olive oil
- ½ red onion
- 2 eggs
- ¼ tsp salt
- 2 oz. cheddar cheese
- 1 garlic clove
- ¼ tsp dill

DIRECTIONS

1. In a skillet sauté kale until tender
2. In a bowl whisk eggs with salt and cheese
3. In a frying pan heat olive oil and pour egg mixture
4. Add remaining ingredients and mix well
5. When ready serve with sautéed kale

JICAMA FRITATTA

Serves: 2

Prep Time: **10** Minutes

Cook Time: **20** Minutes

Total Time: **30** Minutes

INGREDIENTS

- ½ cup jicama
- 1 tablespoon olive oil
- ½ red onion
- 2 eggs
- ¼ tsp salt
- 2 oz. parmesan cheese
- 1 garlic clove
- ¼ tsp dill

DIRECTIONS

1. In a bowl whisk eggs with salt and parmesan cheese
2. In a frying pan heat olive oil and pour egg mixture
3. Add remaining ingredients and mix well
4. Serve when ready

BROCCOLI FRITATTA

Serves: 2

Prep Time: 10 Minutes

Cook Time: 20 Minutes

Total Time: 30 Minutes

INGREDIENTS

- 1 cup broccoli
- 1 tablespoon olive oil
- ½ red onion
- 2 eggs
- ¼ tsp salt
- 2 oz. cheddar cheese
- 1 garlic clove
- ¼ tsp dill

DIRECTIONS

1. In a skillet sauté broccoli until tender
2. In a bowl whisk eggs with salt and cheese
3. In a frying pan heat olive oil and pour egg mixture
4. Add remaining ingredients and mix well
5. When ready serve with sautéed broccoli

CAULIFLOWER SANDWICH

Serves: **2**

Prep Time: **10** Minutes

Cook Time: **30** Minutes

Total Time: **40** Minutes

INGREDIENTS

- **1 head cauliflower**
- **4 tablespoons olive oil**
- **¼ tsp salt**
- **½ red onion**
- **2 tablespoons tahini**
- **1 clove garlic**
- **4 slices gluten-free bread**
- **1 avocado**

DIRECTIONS

1. Toss the cauliflower with olive oil and roast at 400 F for 22-25 minutes
2. In a saucepan sauté the onion until soft
3. Add roasted cauliflower, tahini, olive oil, salt and cook for 1-2 minutes
4. Place everything in a blender and blend until smooth
5. Spread mixture over bread slices

AVOCADO BOATS

Serves: **2**

Prep Time: **10** Minutes

Cook Time: **10** Minutes

Total Time: **20** Minutes

INGREDIENTS

- 1 can chickpeas
- ¼ red onion
- ¼ tsp turmeric
- 1 tablespoon dill
- ½ tsp garlic powder
- 1 tablespoon mustard
- ½ cup tahini
- 2 avocados

DIRECTIONS

1. Cut avocado in half and scoop out part of the interior
2. In a bowl combine together chickpeas with onion, turmeric, dill, garlic, tahini and mustard
3. Mix well and spoon mixture into avocado halves
4. Serve when ready

MEXICAN CORN DIP

Serves: **2**

Prep Time: **10** Minutes

Cook Time: **20** Minutes

Total Time: **30** Minutes

INGREDIENTS

- 2 cups kernels
- 1 tablespoon butter
- 1 jalapeno pepper
- 1 tsp chili powder
- 1 red onion
- ½ cup mayonnaise
- 1 tablespoon lime juice
- 2 tablespoons cilantro

DIRECTIONS

1. In a skillet melt butter over medium heat
2. Add corn and cook for 5-6 minutes
3. Add chili powder, jalapeno, red onion and cook on low heat
4. Add lime juice, mayonnaise and cook for another 2-3 minutes
5. Remove from heat, stir in cilantro and serve with tortilla chips

LEEK QUICHE

Serves: **4**

Prep Time: **10** Minutes

Cook Time: **50** Minutes

Total Time: **60** Minutes

INGREDIENTS

- 1 tablespoon butter
- 1 bunch asparagus
- 1 leek
- ¼ tsp salt
- 2 eggs
- ½ cup vanilla yogurt
- 1 cup almond milk
- 1 cup cheese
- 1 pie crust

DIRECTIONS

1. In a saucepan melt butter, add leek, asparagus, pepper, salt and cook until vegetables are soft
2. In a bowl combine eggs, milk, yogurt and mix well
3. Place egg mixture on the pie crust
4. Top with asparagus and leek
5. Bake at 375 F for 40-45 minutes, when ready remove and serve

ROASTED SQUASH

Serves: **3-4**

Prep Time: **10** Minutes

Cook Time: **20** Minutes

Total Time: **30** Minutes

INGREDIENTS

- 2 delicata squashes
- 2 tablespoons olive oil
- 1 tsp curry powder
- 1 tsp salt

DIRECTIONS

1. Preheat the oven to 400 F
2. Cut everything in half lengthwise
3. Toss everything with olive oil and place onto a prepared baking sheet
4. Roast for 18-20 minutes at 400 F or until golden brown
5. When ready remove from the oven and serve

BRUSSELS SPROUT CHIPS

Serves: 2
Prep Time: 10 Minutes
Cook Time: 20 Minutes
Total Time: 30 Minutes

INGREDIENTS

- 1 lb. brussels sprouts
- 1 tablespoon olive oil
- 1 tablespoon parmesan cheese
- 1 tsp garlic powder
- 1 tsp seasoning

DIRECTIONS

1. Preheat the oven to 425 F
2. In a bowl toss everything with olive oil and seasoning
3. Spread everything onto a prepared baking sheet
4. Bake for 8-10 minutes or until crisp
5. When ready remove from the oven and serve

CUCUMBER CHIPS

Serves: 2

Prep Time: 10 Minutes

Cook Time: 20 Minutes

Total Time: 30 Minutes

INGREDIENTS

- 1 lb. cucumber
- 1 tsp salt
- 1 tsp smoked paprika
- 1 tablespoon olive oil

DIRECTIONS

1. Preheat the oven to 425 F
2. In a bowl toss everything with olive oil and seasoning
3. Spread everything onto a prepared baking sheet
4. Bake for 8-10 minutes or until crisp
5. When ready remove from the oven and serve

SQUASH CHIPS

Serves: 2
Prep Time: 10 Minutes
Cook Time: 20 Minutes
Total Time: 30 Minutes

INGREDIENTS

- 1 lb. squash
- 1 tsp salt
- 1 tsp smoked paprika
- 1 tablespoon olive oil

DIRECTIONS

1. Preheat the oven to 425 F
2. In a bowl toss everything with olive oil and seasoning
3. Spread everything onto a prepared baking sheet
4. Bake for 8-10 minutes or until crisp
5. When ready remove from the oven and serve

PASTA

SIMPLE SPAGHETTI

Serves: 2
Prep Time: 5 Minutes
Cook Time: 15 Minutes
Total Time: 20 Minutes

INGREDIENTS

- 10 oz. spaghetti
- 2 eggs
- ½ cup parmesan cheese
- 1 tsp black pepper
- Olive oil
- 1 tsp parsley
- 2 cloves garlic

DIRECTIONS

1. In a pot boil spaghetti (or any other type of pasta), drain and set aside
2. In a bowl whisk eggs with parmesan cheese
3. In a skillet heat olive oil, add garlic and cook for 1-2 minutes
4. Pour egg mixture and mix well
5. Add pasta and stir well

6. When ready garnish with parsley and serve

SHRIMP PASTA

Serves: 2
Prep Time: 5 Minutes
Cook Time: 15 Minutes
Total Time: 20 Minutes

INGREDIENTS

- ¼ cup mayonnaise
- ¼ cup sweet chili sauce
- 1 tablespoon lime juice
- 1 garlic clove
- 8 z. pasta
- 1 lb. shrimp
- ¼ tsp paprika

DIRECTIONS

1. In a pot boil spaghetti (or any other type of pasta), drain and set aside
2. Place all the ingredients for the sauce in a pot and bring to a simmer
3. Add pasta and mix well
4. When ready garnish with parmesan cheese and serve

PASTA WITH OLIVES AND TOMATOES

Serves: 2
Prep Time: 5 Minutes
Cook Time: 15 Minutes
Total Time: 20 Minutes

INGREDIENTS

- 8 oz. pasta
- 3 tablespoons olive oil
- 2 cloves garlic
- 5-6 anchovy fillets
- 2 cups tomatoes
- 1 cup olives
- ½ cup basil leaves

DIRECTIONS

1. In a pot boil spaghetti (or any other type of pasta), drain and set aside
2. Place all the ingredients for the sauce in a pot and bring to a simmer
3. Add pasta and mix well
4. When ready garnish with parmesan cheese and serve

SALAD

MORNING SALAD

Serves: **2**
Prep Time: **5** Minutes
Cook Time: **5** Minutes
Total Time: **10** Minutes

INGREDIENTS

- 1 onion
- 1 tsp cumin
- 1 tablespoon olive oil
- 1 avocado
- ¼ lb. cooked lentils
- 1 oz. walnuts
- Coriander
- ¼ lb. feta cheese
- Salad dressing of choice
- 8-10 baby carrots

DIRECTIONS

1. **In a bowl combine all ingredients together and mix well**
2. **Add dressing and serve**

TOMATO SOUP

Serves: **1**

Prep Time: **5** Minutes

Cook Time: **10** Minutes

Total Time: **15** Minutes

INGREDIENTS

- ¾ cup chicken broth
- 2 tbs tomato paste
- 2 tbs milk
- ½ cup tomatoes
- 1 tbs vinegar
- 1 tbs onion
- 1 clove garlic
- 1 tsp oregano
- Salt
- Pepper
- Basil leaves

DIRECTIONS

1. Pulse the ingredients in a food processor, saving the basil for garnish.
2. Cook the mixture until heated.
3. Serve garnished with basil leaves and toast.

CRAB SALAD

Serves: **1**

Prep Time: **5** Minutes

Cook Time: **10** Minutes

Total Time: **15** Minutes

INGREDIENTS

- ½ cup celery
- 1 tbs vinegar
- 1 tsp seasoning
- 100 g crab
- Red pepper flakes
- 2 tbs lemon juice
- 2 tbs onion

DIRECTIONS

1. Sauté the ingredients in a pan until celery is tender.
2. Season to taste.
3. Serve when ready

ASIAN SALAD

Serves: **1**

Prep Time: **5** Minutes

Cook Time: **5** Minutes

Total Time: **10** Minutes

INGREDIENTS

- ½ cup orange segments
- 1 packet stevia
- 1 toast
- 100g chicken breast
- ¼ tsp salt
- Orange citrus dressing
- 2 cups romaine lettuce

DIRECTIONS

1. Cook the chicken in a skillet until golden.
2. Combine all of the ingredients in a bowl.
3. Serve immediately.

CHICKEN SALAD

Serves: **1**

Prep Time: **5** Minutes

Cook Time: **10** Minutes

Total Time: **15** Minutes

INGREDIENTS

- 100g chicken
- ½ tsp onion powder
- ½ tsp garlic powder
- ½ tsp oregano
- 1 tsp paprika
- ½ tsp thyme
- ½ tsp black pepper
- ¼ tsp salad greens

DIRECTIONS

1. Rub the chicken with the combined spices.
2. Grill the pink until golden.
3. Serve over the salad greens and desired dressing.

CUCUMBER SALAD

Serves: *1*

Prep Time: *5* Minutes

Cook Time: *0* Minutes

Total Time: *5* Minutes

INGREDIENTS

- ¼ tsp salt
- 2 tsp parsley
- ¼ cup vinegar
- 2 tsp green onion
- Pepper
- Stevia
- 1 cucumber

DIRECTIONS

1. Chop the cucumber.
2. Mix the ingredients in a bowl.
3. Refrigerate for at least 10 minutes, then serve.

GRAPEFRUIT SALAD

Serves: **1**

Prep Time: **10** Minutes

Cook Time: **0** Minutes

Total Time: **10** Minutes

INGREDIENTS

- 2 tbs apple vinegar
- Grapefruit juice
- ½ tsp ginger
- Salt
- 1 red grapefruit
- 1 cucumber
- Pepper
- Cilantro
- 2 tbs onion
- Ruby red dressing

DIRECTIONS

1. Peel the grapefruit and cut it into cubes.
2. Mix with the rest of the ingredients and season.
3. Serve topped with red dressing.

APPLE SALAD

Serves: 2

Prep Time: 5 Minutes

Cook Time: 0 Minutes

Total Time: 5 Minutes

INGREDIENTS

- ½ cup green apple
- 1 tbs lemon juice
- Salt
- Pepper
- Stevia
- ½ cup cucumber
- 2 tbs apple cider vinegar

DIRECTIONS

1. Chop the apple and cucumber.
2. Combine the ingredients and add stevia.
3. Serve immediately.

COLESLAW

Serves: **1**

Prep Time: **10** Minutes

Cook Time: **0** Minutes

Total Time: **10** Minutes

INGREDIENTS

- 1 ½ cups cabbage
- ¼ tsp onion powder
- Cayenne pepper
- Salt
- Pepper
- 2 tbs vinegar
- 2 tbs lemon juice
- 1 tsp horseradish
- 1 clove garlic
- ½ tsp mustard

DIRECTIONS

1. Slice the cabbage.
2. Mix the rest of the ingredients in a bowl.
3. Pour the mixture over the cabbage and serve.

LOBSTER SALAD

Serves: *1*

Prep Time: *5* Minutes

Cook Time: *5* Minutes

Total Time: *10* Minutes

INGREDIENTS

- 100g lobster
- 1 serving Tarragon Vinaigrette
- 2 tbs lemon juice
- 1 tbs tarragon
- ½ tsp garlic powder
- 2 tbs onion
- 1 tbs green onion

DIRECTIONS

1. Cook the lobster.
2. Sauté the lobster, lemon juice, green onion, onion, tarragon, garlic powder, salt, and pepper until onion is tender.
3. Top the lettuce with the lobster mixture.
4. Serve topped with Tarragon Vinaigrette.

RADISH SALAD

Serves: 1
Prep Time: 10 Minutes
Cook Time: 20 Minutes
Total Time: 30 Minutes

INGREDIENTS

- 2 tbs lemon juice
- 1 tbs onion
- 1 tbs parsley
- Salt
- Radishes
- Pepper

DIRECTIONS

1. Combine all of the ingredients in a bowl.
2. Refrigerate for at least 20 minutes.
3. Serve.

SPINACH SALAD

Serves: **1**

Prep Time: **5** Minutes

Cook Time: **5** Minutes

Total Time: **10** Minutes

INGREDIENTS

- 1 bunch spinach
- Pepper
- Mint leaves
- 2 tbs vinegar
- 2 tbs lemon juice
- 5 strawberries
- ¼ tsp Stevia
- Salt

DIRECTIONS

1. Blend 2 strawberries, lemon juice, vinegar, Stevia, salt, and pepper together.
2. Pour the dressing over the salad and the sliced remained strawberry.
3. Serve topped with mint leaves.

FOURTH COOKBOOK

SOUP RECIPES

CAULIFLOWER SOUP

Serves: **4**

Prep Time: **10** Minutes

Cook Time: **20** Minutes

Total Time: **30** Minutes

INGREDIENTS

- 1 tablespoon olive oil
- 1 lb. cauliflower
- ¼ red onion
- ½ cup all-purpose flour
- ¼ tsp salt
- ¼ tsp pepper
- 1 can vegetable broth
- 1 cup heavy cream

DIRECTIONS

1. In a saucepan heat olive oil and sauté cauliflower until tender
2. Add remaining ingredients to the saucepan and bring to a boil
3. When all the vegetables are tender transfer to a blender and blend until smooth
4. Pour soup into bowls, garnish with parsley and serve

MUSHROOM SOUP

Serves: **4**

Prep Time: **10** Minutes

Cook Time: **30** Minutes

Total Time: **40** Minutes

INGREDIENTS

- 2 tablespoons unsalted butter
- ½ cup minced onion
- ½ cup mushrooms
- 2 tablespoons all-purpose flour
- ¼ cup low sodium chicken broth
- ¼ cup almond milk
- pepper

DIRECTIONS

1. In a soup pot add all soup ingredients
2. Sauté for 5-6 minutes
3. Add water simmer for 20-30 minutes
4. Season with pepper
5. When ready, pour into bowls and serve

ZUCCHINI SOUP

Serves: **4**

Prep Time: **10** Minutes

Cook Time: **20** Minutes

Total Time: **30** Minutes

INGREDIENTS

- 1 tablespoon olive oil
- 1 lb. zucchini
- ¼ red onion
- ½ cup all-purpose flour
- ¼ tsp salt
- ¼ tsp pepper
- 1 can vegetable broth
- 1 cup heavy cream

DIRECTIONS

1. In a saucepan heat olive oil and sauté zucchini until tender
2. Add remaining ingredients to the saucepan and bring to a boil
3. When all the vegetables are tender transfer to a blender and blend until smooth
4. Pour soup into bowls, garnish with parsley and serve

CELERY SOUP

Serves: **4**

Prep Time: **10** Minutes

Cook Time: **20** Minutes

Total Time: **30** Minutes

INGREDIENTS

- 1 tablespoon olive oil
- 1 lb. celery
- ¼ red onion
- ½ cup all-purpose flour
- ¼ tsp salt
- ¼ tsp pepper
- 1 can vegetable broth
- 1 cup heavy cream

DIRECTIONS

1. In a saucepan heat olive oil and sauté celery until tender
2. Add remaining ingredients to the saucepan and bring to a boil
3. When all the vegetables are tender transfer to a blender and blend until smooth
4. Pour soup into bowls, garnish with parsley and serve

CARROT SOUP

Serves: **4**

Prep Time: **10** Minutes

Cook Time: **20** Minutes

Total Time: **30** Minutes

INGREDIENTS

- 1 tablespoon olive oil
- 1 lb. carrots
- ¼ red onion
- ½ cup all-purpose flour
- ¼ tsp salt
- ¼ tsp pepper
- 1 can vegetable broth
- 1 cup heavy cream

DIRECTIONS

1. In a saucepan heat olive oil and sauté carrots until tender
2. Add remaining ingredients to the saucepan and bring to a boil
3. When all the vegetables are tender transfer to a blender and blend until smooth
4. Pour soup into bowls, garnish with parsley and serve

CUCUMBER SOUP

Serves: **4**

Prep Time: **10** Minutes

Cook Time: **20** Minutes

Total Time: **30** Minutes

INGREDIENTS

- 1 tablespoon olive oil
- 1 lb. cucumber
- ¼ red onion
- ½ cup all-purpose flour
- ¼ tsp salt
- ¼ tsp pepper
- 1 can vegetable broth
- 1 cup heavy cream

DIRECTIONS

1. In a saucepan heat olive oil and sauté cucumber until tender
2. Add remaining ingredients to the saucepan and bring to a boil
3. When all the vegetables are tender transfer to a blender and blend until smooth
4. Pour soup into bowls, garnish with parsley and serve

SIDE DISHES

GOAT'S CHEESE RAREBIT

Serves: **4**

Prep Time: **10** Minutes

Cook Time: **30** Minutes

Total Time: **40** Minutes

INGREDIENTS

- 1 oz. olive oil
- 150 ml soya milk
- 6 oz. goat cheese
- 1 oz. flour
- ½ tsp mustard
- pepper
- 1 egg yolk
- 4 bread slices

DIRECTIONS

1. In a saucepan add butter, cheese, soya milk and cook on low heat
2. Stir in flour and bring mixture to a boil
3. Remove from heat add mustard, pepper and whisk in the egg yolks
4. Toast the bread and spread mixture between the slices

5. Place on a grill and cook until golden brown

SMOKED MACKEREL PATE

Serves: **2**

Prep Time: **10** Minutes

Cook Time: **10** Minutes

Total Time: **20** Minutes

INGREDIENTS

- 7 oz. smoked mackerel fillets
- 2 onions
- 1 lemon
- 3 oz. cream cheese
- 1 tablespoon creamed horseradish
- pepper

DIRECTIONS

1. Cut mackerel into small chunks
2. In a bowl mix cream cheese, mackerel, creamed horseradish, onions and zest of 1 lemon
3. Mix with lemon juice and season with pepper and pate that should be ready

PESTO CREAM VEGGIE DIP

Serves: **4**

Prep Time: **10** Minutes

Cook Time: **30** Minutes

Total Time: **40** Minutes

INGREDIENTS

- 7 oz. basil pesto
- 3 oz. cream cheese
- 3 oz. sour cream
- 2 tablespoons parmesan cheese

DIRECTIONS

1. In a bowl add cream cheese, pesto, sour cream and parmesan cheese
2. Mix well and serve when ready

CAULIFLOWER CHEESE

Serves: **6**

Prep Time: **10** Minutes

Cook Time: **20** Minutes

Total Time: **30** Minutes

INGREDIENTS

- 1 cauliflower
- 500 ml milk
- 3 tablespoons flour
- 2 oz. butter
- 3 oz. cheddar cheese
- 2 tablespoons breadcrumbs

DIRECTIONS

1. Preheat the oven to 400 F
2. In a saucepan add cauliflower and cook for 5-8 minutes
3. Add milk, butter, flour and whisk until mixture boils
4. Stir in cheese and pour over the cauliflower
5. Scatter over the remaining cheese and breadcrumbs
6. Bake cauliflower cheese for 18-20 minutes

PUMPKIN RISOTTO

Serves: **4**

Prep Time: **10** Minutes

Cook Time: **30** Minutes

Total Time: **40** Minutes

INGREDIENTS

- 2 tablespoons olive oil
- 1 onion
- 500 ml chicken stock
- 10 sage leaves
- 6 oz. Arborio rice
- 9 oz. pumpkin
- 2 oz. butter
- 1 pinch black pepper
- parmesan cheese

DIRECTIONS

1. In a saucepan add ½ chicken stock and cook on low heat, add sage, onion, rice and continue to simmer
2. Add pumpkin, remaining stock and cook until stock is absorbed and pumpkin is soft
3. Stir in butter, season with pepper and divide into 2-3 servings
4. Add grated cheese and serve

GREEN PESTO PASTA

Serves: **2**

Prep Time: **5** Minutes

Cook Time: **15** Minutes

Total Time: **20** Minutes

INGREDIENTS

- 4 oz. spaghetti
- 2 cups basil leaves
- 2 garlic cloves
- ¼ cup olive oil
- 2 tablespoons parmesan cheese
- ½ tsp black pepper

DIRECTIONS

7. **Bring water to a boil and add pasta**
8. **In a blend add parmesan cheese, basil leaves, garlic and blend**
9. **Add olive oil, pepper and blend again**
10. **Pour pesto onto pasta and serve when ready**

MINCE WITH BASIL

Serves: **4**

Prep Time: **10** Minutes

Cook Time: **20** Minutes

Total Time: **30** Minutes

INGREDIENTS

- 1 lb. beef
- 1 garlic clove
- 1 chili
- 1 onion
- 1 oz. fresh basil
- 1 tablespoon soy sauce
- 1 tablespoon vegetable oil

DIRECTIONS

1. Fry garlic, chili and mince over medium heat
2. Add the rest of ingredients and cook for 18-20 minutes
3. Remove from heat and serve with rice

PORK CHOPS

Serves: **4**

Prep Time: **10** Minutes

Cook Time: **30** Minutes

Total Time: **40** Minutes

INGREDIENTS

- 2 pork chops
- 1 tsp mustard
- 1 tsp oil
- 1 spring onion
- 1 clove garlic
- 1 tablespoon breadcrumbs
- 1 pinch dried hers

DIRECTIONS

1. Preheat the oven to 375 F
2. Spread the mustard over the pork chop
3. In a bowl add garlic, dried herbs, breadcrumbs, onions and mix well
4. Spread the herb mixture on top of each pork chop
5. Bake for 20-25 minutes
6. Remove and serve with boiled potatoes

BEEF BURGERS

Serves: **4**

Prep Time: **10** Minutes

Cook Time: **20** Minutes

Total Time: **30** Minutes

INGREDIENTS

- 1 lb. minced beef
- 1 onion
- 1 pinch dried herb
- 1 pinch black pepper

DIRECTIONS

1. Preheat the grill to hot
2. In a bowl mix all ingredients together
3. Divide mixture into 4 portion and shape into patties
4. Grill for 5-6 minutes per side or until brown
5. Serve in a burger bun with potato fries

BAKED FISH

Serves: **4**

Prep Time: **10** Minutes

Cook Time: **30** Minutes

Total Time: **40** Minutes

INGREDIENTS

- 1 lb. boneless fish fillets
- juice of 1 lemon
- 1 tablespoon unsalted butter
- 1 pinch rosemary

DIRECTIONS

1. Preheat the oven to 325 F
2. Place the fish in a shallow baking dish
3. In a bowl mix all remaining ingredients
4. Dot over fish fillets
5. Bake for 25 minutes or until fish is tender
6. Serve with vegetables

MINT COUSCOUS

Serves: **4**

Prep Time: **10** Minutes

Cook Time: **15** Minutes

Total Time: **25** Minutes

INGREDIENTS

- ½ lb. couscous
- 500 ml water
- 2 tablespoons mint
- 2 teaspoons olive oil

DIRECTIONS

1. In a saucepan bring water to a boil
2. Add couscous and cover with a lid
3. Drizzle oil, mint and cook until soft
4. Season with black pepper and serve with baked fish

FRESH PORK PATTIES

Serves: **8**
Prep Time: **10** minutes
Cook Time: **20** minutes
Total Time: **30** minutes

INGREDIENTS

- 2 lbs fresh lean ground pork
- ½ teaspoon black pepper
- 1 teaspoon lemon juice
- ½ teaspoon ground sage
- ½ teaspoon marjoram
- 1 teaspoon paprika

DIRECTIONS

1. Combine all ingredients in a bowl and mix them
2. Add 2-3 tablespoons water to the pork mixture and mix
3. Form into 8 patties
4. Spray skillet with cooking spray
5. Sprinkle the patties with paprika
6. Cook until crispy brown
7. Remove excess fat
8. Cooked pork patties can be frozen for later if you want

POTATO SALAD

Serves: 2

Prep Time: 5 Minutes

Cook Time: 5 Minutes

Total Time: 10 Minutes

INGREDIENTS

- 2 lb. cooked red potatoes
- 1 tablespoon salt
- ¼ cup olive oil
- ¼ cup parsley
- ¼ cup green onions
- 1 tablespoon lemon juice
- 1 tsp mustard
- 2 stalks celery

DIRECTIONS

1. In a bowl mix all ingredients and mix well
2. Serve with dressing

LEBANESE BEAN SALAD

Serves: 2
Prep Time: 5 Minutes
Cook Time: 5 Minutes
Total Time: 10 Minutes

INGREDIENTS

- 1 can black beans
- 1 can chickpeas
- 1 red onion
- 2 stalks celery
- 1 cucumber
- ½ cup parsley
- 1 tablespoon mint
- 2 cloves garlic

DIRECTIONS

1. In a bowl combine all ingredients together and mix well
2. Serve with dressing

KALE & FENNEL SALAD

Serves: 2

Prep Time: 5 Minutes

Cook Time: 5 Minutes

Total Time: 10 Minutes

INGREDIENTS

- 1 bunch kale
- 1 apple
- 1 fennel
- 4 oz. feta cheese
- ½ cup cranberries
- 1 cup maple syrup salad dressing

DIRECTIONS

1. In a bowl combine all ingredients together and mix well
2. Serve with dressing

TOMATO & SPINACH SALAD

Serves: 2

Prep Time: 5 Minutes

Cook Time: 5 Minutes

Total Time: 10 Minutes

INGREDIENTS

- 1 cup quinoa
- 1 cup tomatoes
- 1 cup baby spinach
- 1 tablespoon olive oil
- 1 cup lemon salad dressing

DIRECTIONS

1. In a bowl combine all ingredients together and mix well
2. Serve with dressing

WILD RICE SALAD

Serves: 2
Prep Time: 5 Minutes
Cook Time: 5 Minutes
Total Time: 10 Minutes

INGREDIENTS

- 1 cup cooked wild rice
- 1 tsp olive oil
- 6 oz. arugula
- ¼ cup basil
- ½ cup cranberries
- ½ cup goat cheese
- 1 cup lemon salad dressing

DIRECTIONS

1. In a bowl combine all ingredients together and mix well
2. Serve with dressing

KALE SALAD

Serves: **2**

Prep Time: **5** Minutes

Cook Time: **5** Minutes

Total Time: **10** Minutes

INGREDIENTS

- 1 bunch kale
- 1 cup cooked grains
- 2 carrots
- 1 radish
- 1 tablespoon pepitas
- 1 cup tahini dressing

DIRECTIONS

1. **In a bowl combine all ingredients together and mix well**
2. **Serve with dressing**

THAI MANGO SALAD

Serves: 2
Prep Time: 5 Minutes
Cook Time: 5 Minutes
Total Time: 10 Minutes

INGREDIENTS

- 1 head leaf lettuce
- 1 red bell pepper
- 2 mangoes
- 1 cup green onion
- ½ cup peanuts
- ½ cup cilantro
- 1 cup peanut dressing

DIRECTIONS

1. In a bowl combine all ingredients together and mix well
2. Serve with dressing

HERBED SALAD

Serves: 2
Prep Time: 5 Minutes
Cook Time: 5 Minutes
Total Time: 10 Minutes

INGREDIENTS

- 2 lb. cooked white potatoes
- 2 tablespoons olive oil
- ½ cup parsley
- ½ cup green onion
- 1 tablespoon lemon juice
- 1 tsp mustard
- 2 cloves garlic
- 1 tsp black pepper
- 1 tsp oregano

DIRECTIONS

1. In a bowl combine all ingredients together and mix well
2. Serve with dressing

BEET SALAD

Serves: 2

Prep Time: 5 Minutes

Cook Time: 5 Minutes

Total Time: 10 Minutes

INGREDIENTS

- 1 cup cooked quinoa
- 1 cup edamame
- 1 cup pepitas
- 1 beet
- 1 carrot
- 1 cup baby spinach
- 1 avocado
- 1 cup lemon salad dressing

DIRECTIONS

1. In a bowl combine all ingredients together and mix well
2. Serve with dressing

PEPITAS AND CRANBERRIES SALAD

Serves: 2
Prep Time: 5 Minutes
Cook Time: 5 Minutes
Total Time: 10 Minutes

INGREDIENTS

- 6 oz. greens
- 1 apple
- 1 cup cranberries
- ½ cup pepitas
- 3 oz. feta cheese

DIRECTIONS

1. **In a bowl combine all ingredients together and mix well**
2. **Serve with dressing**

FIESTA SHRIMP

Serves: 1
Prep Time: 5 Minutes
Cook Time: 10 Minutes
Total Time: 15 Minutes

INGREDIENTS

- 3 oz. shrimp
- ¼ cup zucchini
- ½ cup fiesta garden salsa
- ¼ oz. cheese
- cilantro
- 1 tortilla

DIRECTIONS

1. In a bowl add zucchini, shrimp and pour salsa over
2. Microwave for 4-5 minutes and sprinkle with grated cheese and cilantro
3. Microwave tortilla for 10-20 seconds and serve with shrimp

CAULIFLOWER FRITTERS

Serves: **8**

Prep Time: **10** Minutes

Cook Time: **30** Minutes

Total Time: **40** Minutes

INGREDIENTS

- 1 head of cauliflower
- ¼ tsp chili powder
- 2 cloves garlic
- 2 tablespoons cilantro
- 1 tsp salt
- ¼ tsp black pepper
- 2 eggs
- 3 tablespoons cornmeal
- ½ cup flour
- 4 tablespoons nutritional yeast

DIRECTIONS

1. Cook cauliflower florets by steaming for 5-6 minutes
2. Mix the cauliflower with chili powder, cilantro, garlic, pepper and salt
3. In another bowl beat the egg, add cauliflower mixture, flour, cornmeal, and yeast

4. Add ¼ cup of the mixture to the pan and press down the fritter
5. Cook until golden brown for 3-4 minutes per side
6. When ready, remove and serve

FRENCH TOAST SANDWICHES

Serves: 2

Prep Time: 5 Minutes

Cook Time: 10 Minutes

Total Time: 15 Minutes

INGREDIENTS

- 4 thin slices bread
- 2 eggs
- 1/3 cup almond milk
- ¼ tsp vanilla extract
- 1 tablespoon cream cheese
- 1 tablespoon apricot preserves
- ½ cup maple syrup

DIRECTIONS

1. In a bowl combine vanilla extract, eggs, almond milk, and mix well
2. Make 2 sandwiches with cream cheese and preserve
3. Place sandwiches in egg mixture on both sides
4. In a skillet cook sandwiches for 2-3 minutes per side or until golden brown
5. When ready remove and serve

GREEK MIXED VEGETABLES

Serves: **6**

Prep Time: **10** Minutes

Cook Time: **90** Minutes

Total Time: **100** Minutes

INGREDIENTS

- ½ cup olive oil
- 1 eggplant
- 1 onion
- 2 garlic cloves
- 1 lb. potatoes
- 5 tomatoes
- 10 cherry tomatoes
- 1 cup tomato passata
- 1 cup water
- 1 tablespoon dried oregano
- 1 tablespoon parsley
- 1 tsp salt

DIRECTIONS

1. Preheat the oven to 400 F
2. In a frying pan add olive oil, eggplant and cook for 6-7 minutes

3. Add garlic, onion and sauté for 5-6 minutes
4. Add potato, zucchini, passata, tomatoes, and water
5. Sprinkle with oregano, parsley, pepper, and salt
6. Mix well and transfer to a baking dish, drizzle with olive oil and bake for 45-55 minutes or until the top has browned
7. When ready remove and serve

GRILLED SALMON STEAKS

Serves: **4**

Prep Time: **5** Minutes

Cook Time: **15** Minutes

Total Time: **20** Minutes

INGREDIENTS

- 2 salmon steaks
- 2 tablespoons dipping sauce
- 1 tsp cooking oil

DIRECTIONS

1. Heat grill and rub with cooking oil
2. Baste steaks with sauce
3. Cook for 4-5 minutes per side
4. Don't overcook
5. When ready remove and serve

ORIENTAL GREENS

Serves: **8**

Prep Time: **10** Minutes

Cook Time: **90** Minutes

Total Time: **100** Minutes

INGREDIENTS

- ¼ cup green beans
- ¼ cup snow peas
- 1 cup cauliflower florets
- 1 cup water chestnuts
- 2 radishes
- 2 scallions
- ½ cup red onion
- 1 tsp powdered ginger
- ½ cup rice wine vinegar

DIRECTIONS

1. In a bowl combine cauliflower floret, radish slices, onions, water chestnuts and mix well
2. In another bowl combine rice wine vinegar, powdered ginger and pour over vegetables
3. Refrigerate for 1-2 hours
4. When ready remove and serve

BROCCOLI CASSEROLE

Serves: **4**

Prep Time: **10** Minutes

Cook Time: **15** Minutes

Total Time: **25** Minutes

INGREDIENTS

- 1 onion
- 2 chicken breasts
- 2 tablespoons unsalted butter
- 2 eggs
- 2 cups cooked rice
- 2 cups cheese
- 1 cup parmesan cheese
- 2 cups cooked broccoli

DIRECTIONS

1. Sauté the veggies and set aside
2. Preheat the oven to 425 F
3. Transfer the sautéed veggies to a baking dish, add remaining ingredients to the baking dish
4. Mix well, add seasoning and place the dish in the oven
5. Bake for 12-15 minutes or until slightly brown
6. When ready remove from the oven and serve

BEAN FRITATTA

Serves: 2

Prep Time: **10** Minutes

Cook Time: **20** Minutes

Total Time: **30** Minutes

INGREDIENTS

- 1 cup black beans
- 1 tablespoon olive oil
- ½ red onion
- 2 eggs
- ¼ tsp salt
- 2 oz. cheddar cheese
- 1 garlic clove
- ¼ tsp dill

DIRECTIONS

5. In a bowl whisk eggs with salt and cheese
6. In a frying pan heat olive oil and pour egg mixture
7. Add remaining ingredients and mix well
8. Serve when ready

ROASTED SQUASH

Serves: **3-4**

Prep Time: **10** Minutes

Cook Time: **20** Minutes

Total Time: **30** Minutes

INGREDIENTS

- 2 delicata squashes
- 2 tablespoons olive oil
- 1 tsp curry powder
- 1 tsp salt

DIRECTIONS

1. Preheat the oven to 400 F
2. Cut everything in half lengthwise
3. Toss everything with olive oil and place onto a prepared baking sheet
4. Roast for 18-20 minutes at 400 F or until golden brown
5. When ready remove from the oven and serve

POTATO CHIPS

Serves: 2

Prep Time: 10 Minutes

Cook Time: 20 Minutes

Total Time: 30 Minutes

INGREDIENTS

- 1 lb. potatoes
- 1 tsp salt
- 1 tsp paprika
- 1 tablespoon olive oil

DIRECTIONS

1. Preheat the oven to 425 F
2. In a bowl toss everything with olive oil and seasoning
3. Spread everything onto a prepared baking sheet
4. Bake for 8-10 minutes or until crisp
5. When ready remove from the oven and serve

PIZZA

ZUCCHINI PIZZA

Serves: **6-8**

Prep Time: **10** Minutes

Cook Time: **15** Minutes

Total Time: **25** Minutes

INGREDIENTS

- 1 pizza crust
- ½ cup tomato sauce
- ¼ black pepper
- 1 cup zucchini slices
- 1 cup mozzarella cheese
- 1 cup olives

DIRECTIONS

1. Spread tomato sauce on the pizza crust
2. Place all the toppings on the pizza crust
3. Bake the pizza at 425 F for 12-15 minutes
4. When ready remove pizza from the oven and serve

TUSCAN PIZZA

Serves: **6-8**

Prep Time: **10** Minutes

Cook Time: **15** Minutes

Total Time: **25** Minutes

INGREDIENTS

- 1 pizza crust
- 200 g prosciutto
- Basil leaves
- 1 cup tomato sauce
- 1 cup mozzarella
- 1 cup tomato slices

DIRECTIONS

1. Spread tomato sauce on the pizza crust
2. Place all the toppings on the pizza crust
3. Bake the pizza at 425 F for 12-15 minutes
4. When ready remove pizza from the oven and serve

MARGHERITA PIZZA

Serves: **6-8**

Prep Time: **10** Minutes

Cook Time: **15** Minutes

Total Time: **25** Minutes

INGREDIENTS

- 1 pizza crust
- 1 cup tomato sauce
- 1 tablespoon olive oil
- 1 cup mozzarella

DIRECTIONS

1. Spread tomato sauce on the pizza crust
2. Place all the toppings on the pizza crust
3. Bake the pizza at 425 F for 12-15 minutes
4. When ready remove pizza from the oven and serve

SHAKSHUKA PIZZA

Serves: **6-8**

Prep Time: **10** Minutes

Cook Time: **15** Minutes

Total Time: **25** Minutes

INGREDIENTS

- 1 pizza crust
- 1 cup marinara sauce
- 1 tsp parprika
- 1 red onion
- 1 cup roasted red peppers
- 1 cup crumbled feta cheese
- 1 cup arugula
- 1 cup mozzarella

DIRECTIONS

1. Spread tomato sauce on the pizza crust
2. Place all the toppings on the pizza crust
3. Bake the pizza at 425 F for 12-15 minutes
4. When ready remove pizza from the oven and serve

FIFTH COOKBOOK

ROAST RECIPES

ROASTED SQUASH

Serves: **3-4**

Prep Time: **10** Minutes

Cook Time: **20** Minutes

Total Time: **30** Minutes

INGREDIENTS

- 2 delicata squashes
- 2 tablespoons olive oil
- 1 tsp curry powder
- 1 tsp salt

DIRECTIONS

1. Preheat the oven to 400 F
2. Cut everything in half lengthwise
3. Toss everything with olive oil and place onto a prepared baking sheet
4. Roast for 18-20 minutes at 400 F or until golden brown
5. When ready remove from the oven and serve

ROASTED CARROT

Serves: **3-4**

Prep Time: **10** Minutes

Cook Time: **20** Minutes

Total Time: **30** Minutes

INGREDIENTS

- 1 lb. carrot
- 2 tablespoons olive oil
- 1 tsp curry powder
- 1 tsp salt

DIRECTIONS

1. Preheat the oven to 400 F
2. Cut everything in half lengthwise
3. Toss everything with olive oil and place onto a prepared baking sheet
4. Roast for 18-20 minutes at 400 F or until golden brown
5. When ready remove from the oven and serve

SOUP RECIPES

ZUCCHINI SOUP

Serves: **4**

Prep Time: **10** Minutes

Cook Time: **20** Minutes

Total Time: **30** Minutes

INGREDIENTS

- 1 tablespoon olive oil
- 1 lb. zucchini
- ¼ red onion
- ½ cup all-purpose flour
- ¼ tsp salt
- ¼ tsp pepper
- 1 can vegetable broth
- 1 cup heavy cream

DIRECTIONS

1. In a saucepan heat olive oil and sauté zucchini until tender
2. Add remaining ingredients to the saucepan and bring to a boil
3. When all the vegetables are tender transfer to a blender and blend until smooth
4. Pour soup into bowls, garnish with parsley and serve

SIDE DISHES

CHICKEN NUGGETS

Serves: 3

Prep Time: 10 Minutes

Cook Time: 25 Minutes

Total Time: 35 Minutes

INGREDIENTS

- 2 chicken breasts
- ¼ cup almond flour
- 1 tablespoon seasoning
- 1 tablespoon olive oil
- ½ tsp salt
- ¼ tsp pepper

DIRECTIONS

1. Preheat the oven to 375 F
2. In a bowl add seasoning, salt, almond flour, pepper
3. Add pieces of chicken breast into your bowl and cover with flour
4. Transfer to your baking sheet
5. Bake 18-20 minutes, remove and serve

BEEF FAJITAS

Serves: **3**

Prep Time: **10** Minutes

Cook Time: **20** Minutes

Total Time: **30** Minutes

INGREDIENTS

- 1 lb. beef stir-fry strips
- 1 red onion
- 1 red bell pepper
- ¼ tsp tsp cumin
- ¼ tsp chili powder
- salt
- pepper
- 1 avocado

DIRECTIONS

1. In a skillet add strips and stir-fry, add salt, pepper and cook for 2-3 minute and set aside
2. Add onions, bell peppers, chili powder, cumin and fry for 2-3 minutes
3. Remove to a plate and serve with avocado

SUMMER SALMON

Serves: **4**

Prep Time: **10** Minutes

Cook Time: **30** Minutes

Total Time: **40** Minutes

INGREDIENTS

- 3 salmon fillets
- 2 leeks
- 6 oz. asparagus spears
- 1 cup sugar snap peas
- 3 tablespoons white wine
- 1 cup vegetable broth
- 1 tablespoon chives
- salt

DIRECTIONS

1. In a Dutch oven add salmon, asparagus, wine, peas, chicken bean and pepper
2. Bring to boil and simmer for 12-15 minutes
3. Sprinkle with chives and serve

GRILLED SALMON

Serves: **4**

Prep Time: **10** Minutes

Cook Time: **20** Minutes

Total Time: **30** Minutes

INGREDIENTS

- Juice of 1 lime
- 2 tablespoons basil
- 3 salmon fillets
- 2 tablespoons salmon fillets
- 2 cup low-fat yogurt
- 1 tablespoon mayonnaise
- ½ tsp lime zest
- salt
- mixed salad leaves

DIRECTIONS

1. In a bowl mix pepper, basil, lime juice, salt and pepper
2. Add salmon fillets and let it marinade for 20-30 minutes
3. In another bowl mix lime zest, basil, mayonnaise, yogurt and salt
4. Preheat the oven to 400 F and place the salmon fillets on a ridged grill pan

5. Brush the salmon with marinade and grill for 4-5 minutes per side
6. When ready remove and serve

MONKFISH MUSSEL KEBABS

Serves: **12**

Prep Time: **10** Minutes

Cook Time: **20** Minutes

Total Time: **30** Minutes

INGREDIENTS

- 1 lemon
- juice 1 lime
- 1 tablespoon olive oil
- 1 tsp honey
- 1 garlic clove
- 1 tablespoon oregano
- 1 tablespoon parsley
- 6 oz. monkfish fillet
- 12 fresh mussels
- 1 yellow bell pepper
- 1 zucchini
- 12 cherry tomatoes
- salt

DIRECTIONS

1. In a bowl add lime juice, honey, lemon zest, garlic, oregano and salt and mix well, marinade for 50-60 minutes

2. Prepare 10-12 wooden skewers and add on each one skewer 1 cube of monkfish, 1 piece of bell pepper, 1 zucchini, 1 mussel and a cherry tomato
3. Grill each kebab for 10-12 minutes or until done
4. When ready, remove and serve

POTATO TORTILLA

Serves: **6**

Prep Time: **10** Minutes

Cook Time: **20** Minutes

Total Time: **30** Minutes

INGREDIENTS

- 1,5 lb. potatoes
- 1 tablespoon olive oil
- 1 red onion
- 1 zucchini
- 1 slice turkey bacon
- 5 eggs
- 1 tablespoon parsley
- pepper

DIRECTIONS

1. In a saucepan add potato cubes, water and bring to a boil
2. In a skillet add potatoes, bacon, zucchini and cook until potatoes are tender
3. In a bowl beat the eggs, add water, pepper, parsley, pour the egg mixture over the vegetables and cook for 4-5 minutes
4. Slide the tortilla onto a plate, cool for 2-3 minutes and cut into wedges and serve

ASIAN STIR-FRY

Serves: 2

Prep Time: 10 Minutes

Cook Time: 10 Minutes

Total Time: 20 Minutes

INGREDIENTS

- ½ lb. dried noodles
- 1 lb. Asian stir-fry vegetables
- ½ cups hoisin sauce
- 1 tsp chili flakes

DIRECTIONS

1. In a frying pan add vegetables, water and stir-fry for 4-5 minutes
2. Add hoisin sauce, noodles, chili flakes and toss to coat, remove and serve

APRICOT CHICKEN PATTIES

Serves: **4**

Prep Time: **10** Minutes

Cook Time: **10** Minutes

Total Time: **20** Minutes

INGREDIENTS

- 1 lb. chicken mince
- 2 slices bread
- 3 oz. pistachio nuts
- 1/3 lb. dried apricots

DIRECTIONS

1. In a bowl mix combine the mince, apricots, bread, pistachios and season with pepper
2. Roll into o4 patties and cook for 4-5 minutes per side
3. Remove and serve

GREEN PESTO PASTA

Serves: 2
Prep Time: 5 Minutes
Cook Time: 15 Minutes
Total Time: 20 Minutes

INGREDIENTS

- 4 oz. spaghetti
- 2 cups basil leaves
- 2 garlic cloves
- ¼ cup olive oil
- 2 tablespoons parmesan cheese
- ½ tsp black pepper

DIRECTIONS

1. Bring water to a boil and add pasta
2. In a blend add parmesan cheese, basil leaves, garlic and blend
3. Add olive oil, pepper and blend again
4. Pour pesto onto pasta and serve when ready

SALMON WITH ROSEMAY

Serves: 2

Prep Time: 10 Minutes

Cook Time: 10 Minutes

Total Time: 20 Minutes

INGREDIENTS

- 3 Atlantic salmon fillets
- 2 tsp olive oil
- 1 clove garlic
- 1 tablespoon rosemary
- black pepper
- 1 tablespoon lemon juice
- 1 tablespoon white wine

DIRECTIONS

1. In a frying pan sauté garlic, rosemary and pepper for 1-2 minutes
2. Add fish and cook for 1-2 minutes per side

MUSHROOM BURGERS

Serves: 2

Prep Time: 10 Minutes

Cook Time: 10 Minutes

Total Time: 20 Minutes

INGREDIENTS

- 2 tablespoons olive oil
- 1 lb. mushrooms
- 1 lb. beef mince
- 1 onion
- 1 tsp Worcestershire sauce
- 1 egg
- 4 hamburger buns
- 1 cup lettuce
- 4 slices tomatoes
- salt

DIRECTIONS

1. In a frying pan add mushrooms and cook for 4-5 minutes, remove and set aside
2. In a bowl mix beef mince, salt, pepper, Worcestershire sauce, mushrooms, onion and mix well
3. Form into 2 patties, and refrigerate for 10-15 minutes

4. In a frying pan cook patty for 2-3 minutes per side and also grill hamburger buns
5. Top buns with lettuce, tomatoes and patties
6. Serve when ready

BLACK BEANS BURGERS

Serves: **4**

Prep Time: **10** Minutes

Cook Time: **20** Minutes

Total Time: **30** Minutes

INGREDIENTS

- 1 lb. black beans
- 1 cup brown rice
- 1 onion
- 1 onion
- ¼ tsp tabasco sauce
- 1 egg
- ½ cup bread crumbs
- 5 tablespoons salsa
- 4 hamburger buns
- ½ cups yoghurt
- 4 leaves romaine lettuce
- 1 avocado

DIRECTIONS

1. **Preheat the oven to 325 F**
2. **In a bowl mix mashed beans, onions, tabasco sauce, rice, egg, breadcrumbs and mix well**

3. Divide mixture into patties and bake for 12-15 minutes or until done
4. In another bowl mix yoghurt and salsa, serve with lettuce and avocado

CABBAGE FRITATTA

Serves: 2
Prep Time: 10 Minutes
Cook Time: 20 Minutes
Total Time: 30 Minutes

INGREDIENTS

- ½ lb. cabbage
- 1 tablespoon olive oil
- ½ red onion
- 2 eggs
- ¼ tsp salt
- 2 oz. cheddar cheese
- 1 garlic clove
- ¼ tsp dill

DIRECTIONS

1. In a bowl whisk eggs with salt and cheese
2. In a frying pan heat olive oil and pour egg mixture
3. Add remaining ingredients and mix well
4. Serve when ready

BRUSSEL SPROUTS FRITATTA

Serves: **2**

Prep Time: **10** Minutes

Cook Time: **20** Minutes

Total Time: **30** Minutes

INGREDIENTS

- ½ lb. Brussel sprouts
- 1 tablespoon olive oil
- ½ red onion
- ¼ tsp salt
- 2 eggs
- 2 oz. cheddar cheese
- 1 garlic clove
- ¼ tsp dill

DIRECTIONS

1. In a skillet sauté Brussel sprouts until tender
2. In a bowl whisk eggs with salt and cheese
3. In a frying pan heat olive oil and pour egg mixture
4. Add remaining ingredients and mix well
5. Serve when ready

CELERY FRITATTA

Serves: 2

Prep Time: 10 Minutes

Cook Time: 20 Minutes

Total Time: 30 Minutes

INGREDIENTS

- 1 cup celery
- 1 tablespoon olive oil
- ½ red onion
- ¼ tsp salt
- 2 eggs
- 2 oz. cheddar cheese
- 1 garlic clove
- ¼ tsp dill

DIRECTIONS

1. In a bowl whisk eggs with salt and cheese
2. In a frying pan heat olive oil and pour egg mixture
3. Add remaining ingredients and mix well
4. When ready serve with sautéed celery

PROSCIUTTO FRITATTA

Serves: 2
Prep Time: 10 Minutes
Cook Time: 20 Minutes
Total Time: 30 Minutes

INGREDIENTS

- 8-10 slices prosciutto
- 1 tsp rosemary
- 1 tablespoon olive oil
- ½ red onion
- ¼ tsp salt
- 2 eggs
- 2 oz. parmesan cheese
- 1 garlic clove
- ¼ tsp dill

DIRECTIONS

1. In a bowl whisk eggs with salt and parmesan cheese
2. In a frying pan heat olive oil and pour egg mixture
3. Add remaining ingredients and mix well
4. When prosciutto and eggs are cooked remove from heat and serve

OREGANO FRITATTA

Serves: 2

Prep Time: 10 Minutes

Cook Time: 20 Minutes

Total Time: 30 Minutes

INGREDIENTS

- 1 tsp oregano
- 1 tablespoon olive oil
- ½ red onion
- ¼ tsp salt
- 2 eggs
- 2 oz. cheddar cheese
- 1 garlic clove
- ¼ tsp dill

DIRECTIONS

1. In a bowl whisk eggs with salt and cheese
2. In a frying pan heat olive oil and pour egg mixture
3. Add remaining ingredients and mix well
4. Serve when ready

HUMMUS WRAP

Serves: 2

Prep Time: 5 Minutes

Cook Time: 5 Minutes

Total Time: 10 Minutes

INGREDIENTS

- 1 cup cooked brown rice
- 1 gluten-free tortilla
- 2-3 tablespoons hummus
- ¼ cup black beans
- ¼ cup tomatoes
- ¼ cup cucumber
- ¼ cup avocado
- ¼ cup romaine lettuce

DIRECTIONS

1. Microwave the tortilla for 20-30 seconds
2. Spread hummus on tortilla
3. Add beans, tomatoes, cucumber, and remaining ingredients
4. Roll like a burrito and serve

POTATO WEDGES

Serves: **4-6**

Prep Time: **10** Minutes

Cook Time: **30** Minutes

Total Time: **40** Minutes

INGREDIENTS

- 2 white potatoes
- 1 tsp olive oil
- 1 tsp garlic powder
- 1 tsp onion powder
- salt
- 1 cup avocado dip

DIRECTIONS

1. Slice potatoes into thick slices
2. In a bowl combine garlic powder, onion powder, salt, olive oil and mix well
3. Place the potatoes into the mixture and stir to coat
4. Bake the potatoes at 425 F for 25-30 minutes
5. When ready remove from the oven and serve with avocado dip

KALE CHIPS

Serves: **4**

Prep Time: **10** Minutes

Cook Time: **15** Minutes

Total Time: **25** Minutes

INGREDIENTS

- 2 cups kale
- 1 tablespoon avocado oil
- 1 tsp salt
- 1 tsp turmeric
- 1 tsp chili powder
- 1 tsp curry powder

DIRECTIONS

1. In a bowl combine all ingredients except kale
2. Mix well and add kale to the seasoning mixture
3. Toss to coat and then place the kale in a baking dish
4. Bake at 250 F for 12-15 minutes
5. When ready remove from the oven and serve

EGG ROLL BOWL

Serves: **2**

Prep Time: **10** Minutes

Cook Time: **20** Minutes

Total Time: **30** Minutes

INGREDIENTS

- 1 tablespoon olive oil
- 1 clove garlic
- 1 lb. pork
- ½ red onion
- 1 cup carrot
- 1 cabbage
- ½ cup soy sauce
- ¼ tsp black pepper

DIRECTIONS

1. In a skillet sauté garlic and onion until soft
2. Add pork, cabbage and cook for another 6-7 minutes
3. Add soy sauce, carrot and cook until vegetables are tender
4. When ready transfer mixture to a bowl, add pepper and serve

GREEK BOWL

Serves: **1**

Prep Time: **10** Minutes

Cook Time: **20** Minutes

Total Time: **30** Minutes

INGREDIENTS

- 1 tablespoon olive oil
- 1 chicken breast
- 1 tsp oregano
- 1 tsp black pepper
- 1 cup tomatoes
- ¼ cucumber
- ¼ cup red onion
- ¼ cup black olives
- 1/4 cup feta cheese
- 1 cup dressing

DIRECTIONS

1. In a skillet add chicken and cook until golden
2. Add seasoning and onion
3. When ready place all ingredients in a bowl
4. Drizzle dressing on top, mix well and serve

CRANBERRY SALAD

Serves: 2

Prep Time: 5 Minutes

Cook Time: 15 Minutes

Total Time: 20 Minutes

INGREDIENTS

- ½ cup celery
- 1 packet Knox Gelatin
- 1 cup cranberry juice
- 1 can berry cranberry sauce
- 1 cup sour cream

DIRECTIONS

1. In a pan add juice, gelatin, cranberry sauce and cook on low heat
2. Add sour cream, celery and continue to cook
3. Pour mixture into a pan
4. Serve when ready

GAZPACHO SALAD

Serves: **4**

Prep Time: **10** Minutes

Cook Time: **30** Minutes

Total Time: **40** Minutes

INGREDIENTS

- ½ lb. cherry tomatoes
- ½ cucumber
- 3 oz. cooked quinoa
- 1 tsp bouillon powder
- 2 spring onions
- 1 red pepper
- ½ avocado
- 1 pack Japanese tofu

DIRECTIONS

1. In a bowl combine all ingredients together
2. Add salad dressing, toss well and serve

RADISH & PARSLEY SALAD

Serves: **4**

Prep Time: **10** Minutes

Cook Time: **30** Minutes

Total Time: **40** Minutes

INGREDIENTS

- 1 tsp olive oil
- ¼ lb. tomatoes
- 2 oz. radish
- 1 oz. parsley
- 1 tablespoon coriander
- salt

DIRECTIONS

1. In a bowl combine all ingredients together and mix well
2. Add salad dressing, toss well and serve

ZUCCHINI & BELL PEPPER SALAD

Serves: **1**

Prep Time: **5** Minutes

Cook Time: **5** Minutes

Total Time: **10** Minutes

INGREDIENTS

- ¼ cup zucchini
- ¼ cup red capsicum
- ½ cup yellow capsicum
- 1 cup sprouted moong
- ¼ cup apple
- 1 tablespoon olive oil
- 1 tsp lemon juice

DIRECTIONS

1. In a bowl combine all ingredients together and mix well
2. Add olive oil, toss well and serve

QUINOA & AVOCADO SALAD

Serves: 1
Prep Time: 5 Minutes
Cook Time: 5 Minutes
Total Time: 10 Minutes

INGREDIENTS

- ¼ cooked quinoa
- ¼ cup avocado
- ¼ cup zucchini
- ¼ cup capsicum cubes
- ¼ cup mushroom
- ½ cup cherry tomatoes
- 1 cup lettuce
- 1 tablespoon sprouts
- 1 tsp olive oil
- Salad dressing

DIRECTIONS

1. In a bowl combine all ingredients together and mix well
2. Add salad dressing, toss well and serve

TOFU SALAD

Serves: **1**

Prep Time: **5** Minutes

Cook Time: **5** Minutes

Total Time: **10** Minutes

INGREDIENTS

- 1 pack tofu
- 1 cup chopped vegetables (carrots, cucumber)

DRESSING

- 1 tablespoon sesame oil
- 1 tablespoon mustard
- 1 tablespoon brown rice vinegar
- 1 tablespoon soya sauce

DIRECTIONS

1. In a bowl combine all ingredients together and mix well
2. Add salad dressing, toss well and serve

PAD THAI SALAD

Serves: 1

Prep Time: 5 Minutes

Cook Time: 5 Minutes

Total Time: 10 Minutes

INGREDIENTS

- ¼ lb. rice noodles
- 1 red pepper
- 1 onion
- 4 stalks coriander
- ¼ package silken tofu
- 1 oz. roasted peanuts
- Salad dressing

DIRECTIONS

1. In a bowl combine all ingredients together and mix well
2. Add salad dressing, toss well and serve

AVOCADO SALAD

Serves: **1**
Prep Time: **5** Minutes
Cook Time: **5** Minutes
Total Time: **10** Minutes

INGREDIENTS

- 2 avocados
- ¼ lb. snap peas
- 1 tablespoon sesame seeds

SALAD DRESSING

- 1 tablespoon soya sauce
- 1 tablespoon umeboshi puree
- 2 tablespoons mikawa mirin

DIRECTIONS

1. In a bowl combine all ingredients together and mix well
2. Add salad dressing, toss well and serve

MUSHROOM SALAD

Serves: **1**

Prep Time: **5** Minutes

Cook Time: **5** Minutes

Total Time: **10** Minutes

INGREDIENTS

- ½ lb. mushrooms
- 1 clove garlic
- ½ lb. salad leaves
- ¼ lb. tofu
- 1 oz. walnuts
- salad dressing

DIRECTIONS

1. In a bowl combine all ingredients together and mix well
2. Add salad dressing, toss well and serve

MIXED GREENS SALAD

Serves: **1**

Prep Time: **5** Minutes

Cook Time: **5** Minutes

Total Time: **10** Minutes

INGREDIENTS

- 2 cucumbers
- 3 radishes
- ¼ red bell pepper
- 2 spring onions
- 1 tablespoon red wine vinegar
- 1 tablespoon rice vinegar
- 1 tablespoon soya sauce
- 1 tablespoon clearspring mirin
- 2 cups mixed salad greens

DIRECTIONS

1. In a bowl combine all ingredients together and mix well
2. Add salad dressing, toss well and serve

QUINOA SALAD

Serves: 1
Prep Time: 5 Minutes
Cook Time: 5 Minutes
Total Time: 10 Minutes

INGREDIENTS

- 1 cup cooked quinoa
- ¼ cup clearspring hijiki
- ¼ red bell pepper
- 1 bun watercress
- 2 radishes
- 2 tablespoons goji berries

DIRECTIONS

1. In a bowl combine all ingredients together and mix well
2. Add salad dressing, toss well and serve

STEW RECIPES

FISH STEW

Serves: **4**

Prep Time: **15** Minutes

Cook Time: **45** Minutes

Total Time: **60** Minutes

INGREDIENTS

- 1 fennel bulb
- 1 red onion
- 2 garlic cloves
- 2 tablespoons olive oil
- 1 cup white wine
- 1 tablespoon fennel seeds
- 4 bay leaves
- 2 cups chicken stock
- 8 oz. halibut
- 12 oz. haddock

DIRECTIONS

1. Chop all ingredients in big chunks
2. In a large pot heat olive oil and add ingredients one by one
3. Cook for 5-6 or until slightly brown

4. Add remaining ingredients and cook until tender, 35-45 minutes
5. Season while stirring on low heat
6. When ready remove from heat and serve

BUTTERNUT SQUASH STEW

Serves: **4**

Prep Time: **15** Minutes

Cook Time: **45** Minutes

Total Time: **60** Minutes

INGREDIENTS

- 2 tablespoons olive oil
- 2 red onions
- 2 cloves garlic
- 1. Tablespoon rosemary
- 1 tablespoon thyme
- 2 lb. beef
- 1 cup white wine
- 1 cup butternut squash
- 2 cups beef broth
- ½ cup tomatoes
-

DIRECTIONS

1. Chop all ingredients in big chunks
2. In a large pot heat olive oil and add ingredients one by one
3. Cook for 5-6 or until slightly brown
4. Add remaining ingredients and cook until tender, 35-45 minutes

5. Season while stirring on low heat
6. When ready remove from heat and serve

CASSEROLE RECIPES

BACON CASSEROLE

Serves: **4**

Prep Time: **10** Minutes

Cook Time: **15** Minutes

Total Time: **25** Minutes

INGREDIENTS

- 4-5 slices bacon
- 3-4 tablespoons butter
- 5-6 tablespoons flour
- 2 cups milk
- 3 cups cheddar cheese
- 2 cups chicken breast
- 1 tsp seasoning mix

DIRECTIONS

1. Sauté the veggies and set aside
2. Preheat the oven to 425 F
3. Transfer the sautéed veggies to a baking dish, add remaining ingredients to the baking dish
4. Mix well, add seasoning and place the dish in the oven
5. Bake for 12-15 minutes or until slightly brown

6. When ready remove from the oven and serve

ENCHILADA CASSEROLE

Serves: **4**

Prep Time: **10** Minutes

Cook Time: **25** Minutes

Total Time: **35** Minutes

INGREDIENTS

- 1 tablespoon olive oil
- 1 red onion
- 1 bell pepper
- 2 cloves garlic
- 1 can black beans
- 1 cup chicken
- 1 can green chilis
- 1 can enchilada sauce
- 1 cup cheddar cheese
- 1 cup sour cream

DIRECTIONS

1. Sauté the veggies and set aside
2. Preheat the oven to 425 F
3. Transfer the sautéed veggies to a baking dish, add remaining ingredients to the baking dish
4. Mix well, add seasoning and place the dish in the oven

5. Bake for 15-25 minutes or until slightly brown
6. When ready remove from the oven and serve

PIZZA RECIPES

CASSEROLE PIZZA

Serves: **6-8**

Prep Time: **10** Minutes

Cook Time: **15** Minutes

Total Time: **25** Minutes

INGREDIENTS

- 1 pizza crust
- ½ cup tomato sauce
- ¼ black pepper
- 1 cup zucchini slices
- 1 cup mozzarella cheese
- 1 cup olives

DIRECTIONS

1. Spread tomato sauce on the pizza crust
2. Place all the toppings on the pizza crust
3. Bake the pizza at 425 F for 12-15 minutes
4. When ready remove pizza from the oven and serve

THANK YOU FOR READING THIS BOOK!

CPSIA information can be obtained
at www.ICGtesting.com
Printed in the USA
BVHW070957010321
601386BV00004B/378

9 781664 033726